Hutchins '98

WICKERBY

WICKERBY

An Urban Pastoral
. . .

CHARLES SIEBERT

Crown Publishers, Inc.
NEW YORK

Portions of this book have appeared in slightly different form in the
following periodicals: *Harper's Magazine, The New York Times Magazine,
Esquire, Outside,* and *Glamour.*

Published by Crown Publishers, Inc., 201 East 50th Street, New York, New York
10022. Member of the Crown Publishing Group.

Random House, Inc. New York, Toronto, London, Sydney, Auckland
www.randomhouse.com

CROWN and colophon are trademarks of Crown Publishers, Inc.

Printed in the United States of America

Design by Lynne Amft

Library of Congress Cataloging-in-Publication Data

Siebert, Charles.
Wickerby : an urban pastoral / Charles Siebert. — 1st ed.
1. Nature. I. Title.
QH81.S59   1998
508—dc21   97-24546
CIP

ISBN 0-609-60237-3

10   9   8   7   6   5   4   3

FOR MY MOTHER, MARION,
AND MY FATHER, CHARLES JOHN.

. . .

I'd like to thank The New York Foundation for the Arts for their generous grant.

Thanks to my agent Chuck Verrill for his guidance and friendship, and to Liz Darhansoff and to Tal Gregory and the entire Darhansoff & Verrill crew.

Though I often cursed her during the rough stretches, I can now thank, wholeheartedly, Abigail Thomas for first prodding me to write a book like *Wickerby*, an undertaking which I would never have completed if not for the deep faith and insight of my editors, Ann Patty and, especially, Elaine Pfefferblit, who stuck with me through her own upheavals to the very end. Thanks go out, as well, to Pat Sheehan for his help and patience, and to the rest of the people at Crown.

I'm grateful to Wickerby's many real-life characters, in particular Mr. J and Albert, to Alan Rabinowitz—aka "El Hombre Tigre"—and to Pat Donadio and the rest of the mumblers over at Pat's Pets.

Fond thanks, of course, to all of Wickerby's human inhabitants, past, present, and future: Freda, Tina and

Checkie; Sophie, John and company; Mike and Mary, Connie, Imogen and Jess; Tony and Carol and Trevor.

To my sisters and brothers: Madeline, Robert, Frances, Catherine, Marion and Joseph, I owe more than they know.

I thank, as well, the many good friends who have heard, read, advised, corrected, encouraged and housed me over the years: Susan, Jeff and Mary, Frank, John and Mary, Nicky, Scott, Jon Lee, Ben, Manny, Gerry, Michael, Lisa, Alan, Will, Eric, Kate, John and Maggie.

To my old Flatlands fireman friend, Pat Featherston, I owe a big thanks for the dubious but ultimately life-affirming gift of my dog, Lucy, who does, I know, miss in her own way, Rasteedy.

And then, of course, there is Bex, to whom I owe everything.

• • •

We soon get through with Nature. She excites an expectation which she cannot satisfy.

HENRY DAVID THOREAU

·THE·
WAY OUT

JUST ACROSS THE STREET from my sixth-story Brooklyn apartment, there's an abandoned apartment inhabited by pigeons. Like me, they have the top-floor place, and looking from my living room, I can see them returning to theirs—hundreds, near dusk, clapping about the windows, resisting the sills in order to land upon them, softly, and then gather themselves into darkening rooms.

All I see here this evening, back now after so many months alone in the woods, are the rooms stacked everywhere into the air around me—millions of windowed squares about to come forward in the twilight for another brief stalemate with the stars. When night fell at Wickerby, the only lights for miles were the cabin's, and I had to be careful then about moving around too much inside because Lucy, my dog, would bark at my reflection in the windowpanes, and I'd be left paralyzed with fear at the thought of who or what in all that darkness might be out there.

Here on the edge of a Brooklyn neighborhood called Crown Heights, gunshots sound nightly, and sirens, and ten-melody car alarms, and riled, drunken conversations from the stoops of the three-story walk-ups down on Lincoln Place, and yet I'll fall fast asleep to all of that tonight, like a child who leaves the bedroom door ajar in order to drift off to the sounds of the company downstairs. At Wickerby, on the other hand, with just woods and sky around me, I'd keep an axe by the bed and lie awake for hours tensed for that first noise I couldn't identify.

Some would say this is a typical city person's sensibility that peoples the open darkness with danger and perversions. But I'm not sure anymore if it was the sordid residue of an urban mind-set that I was arming myself against, or simply the imaginings of an overly isolated one. Whichever, I do know now about the dangers of spending too much time alone. About why lonely people are said to die young, and why hermits are always shown in movies wielding shotguns at the approach of strangers.

Not that loneliness and log cabins are subjects I'd ever hoped to become well versed in. But when circumstances conspire to confine you to a log cabin—when, let's say, the woman you love leaves you to go off on a trip to a remote region of Africa, and, for reasons not entirely, not satisfyingly clear, she doesn't come back when she said she would, and remains out of touch for so long that in response to this and a whole other series of upsets, you suddenly decide to go away yourself, and have as your only refuge a collapsing log cabin that just happens to belong to that woman who left you—then you will, after enough time alone in such a place, notice how everything, your heart, your consciousness, begins to contract, harden, to form a protective shell around the altogether unnatural condition of loneliness. A condition you're soon spending all of yourself defending because it has so readily become you and all that you know.

I just closed up the cabin yesterday for the winter. It's only late September, mild here in Brooklyn this evening, but in Canada the leaves already had that dry rattle on the wind and the nights were getting far too cold to spend within the bare, weakening walls of Wickerby.

If you were to suddenly come upon the place, as I now know hunters do because this spring I found their treetop deer blinds in the nearby woods, or as I imagine cross-country skiers must do in winter along the makeshift trails that traverse the land, then you'd probably assume it to be a long-abandoned ruin and just pass it by.

When Bex first showed me Wickerby six summers ago, our only visit there together, I remember thinking that she had to be out of her mind to have carried on the way she had about the place. Of course, there was a lot that I didn't understand back then about Bex when it came to Wickerby.

Bex—nobody calls her Rebecca anymore except for me when I'm furious at her—is, by nature, an excitable, a capricious woman, "all on the surface," she often says of herself. This means, I've come to understand, not that she's superficial but that very little about her is withheld. That her ever-shifting and unknowable depths are usually right there before you to try and negotiate. And on the subject of Wickerby, I've always found the going to be particularly treacherous.

For long stretches, nothing is said of the place. It doesn't exist. Then, in sudden, tearful tantrums, Bex is claiming it as the one thing from her past of true worth. The one place and time in which she remembers her family being happy. The one place on this earth, as she announced that day six summers ago, that I would, if I really loved her, take her right then and there to see.

Bex drove. Seven hours later, just ten miles or so over the Vermont border into Canada, we were alone in the pitch darkness, our car, with each turn onto the next back road, seeming to shed the world's last patches of pavement and town light until there were just our high beams jiggling over two dirt ruts up a wooded hillside. Albert, the farmer who lives on the hill opposite Wickerby and serves as the cabin's caretaker, had cleared the entrance road a short way in, but then the trees swallowed us whole and from underneath the car there was a loud drumming, like rain on a tin roof, of the tall grass against our manifold. We crested the hill. Bex turned to the right, into an open field, and there, nearly lost among the tall grass stalks and on-going stars, was her Wickerby.

It looked, I told her (she made me apologize for it later), like an abandoned hillbilly shack. It looked, even then, as though it might have but a few more months before it collapsed completely. One rectangular room, about twenty by twenty-five feet, with a simple gable roof, the cabin was built back in the 1840s by homesteaders, who used the stoutest materials. The walls are made of huge, square spruce logs, hand-hewn with an adze and then dovetailed to lock together at the cabin's corners. The roof rafters and cross-beams are all cedar—long, deep red, unfinished logs which, from the inside at least, look and smell as though they were cut just yesterday.

Still, a century and a half of Canadian winters—the deep, slow-rolling waves of freeze and thaw—have rocked the cabin's foundation to the point where the place now looks like an old, weathered houseboat that foundered and broke upon a reef. Daylight leaks in everywhere through the joints and side logs. The floor just inside the front door has a steep, fun-house tilt to it. Most of the louvered window frames have been squeezed permanently shut. A good number of the panes are cracked. And the widening spaces between the logs have been cemented so many times that from the outside, Wickerby resembles a pin-striped mobster's suit.

In the first few weeks of my stay this past spring, I stuffed rolled-up newspapers into all the exposed cracks I could find to help keep the place warm. Rusted tin sheets, meanwhile, that someone nailed long ago over the cabin's old tar-paper roof hold out most of the rain, and the plastic sheets over the broken windows, the wind. And, when nobody's there, a small combination lock on a metal latch holds the front door, barely, within its jamb—or it might be holding the cabin up around the door.

Not that one needs a combination to get inside. At this very moment, all kinds of creatures have the run of the place or, at least, in the increasing cold, the slow, sleepy refuge of its webbed nooks and thinly insulated rafters: mice, moles, snakes, skinks and spiders; bats nesting in the eaves; porcupines gnawing drowsily on the underside of the floorboards. Wickerby is all theirs now, really. I've merely completed a kind of summer time-share with them.

In fact, given the cabin's condition, it's something of a miracle that I managed to last there for the five months that I did, a point that Albert never let me forget. Nearly every evening he'd come up the hill in his red tractor, I think just to see if I was still alive. He'd then remind me what a fool he thought I was to be living in such a place, all the while leading me on the same tour of the cabin's disrepair: the cockeyed front door and the sharply slanted floor just inside it; the numerous breaches in the rock foundation; and finally, the cabin's collapsing south-east corner, where from years of rot and ground shift, one of Wickerby's massive spruce logs is being squeezed, inch by inch, out of position.

There were, I'll admit, some stormy nights over the course of the summer when I would be huddled up in the loft bed with Lucy, riding out the torrents of wind and rain, hearing the downstairs windowpanes crack, waiting for that one corner to finally give way and with it the whole cabin rolling out sideways down the hill like so many Lincoln Logs.

"Gonna go any day," Albert would shout at me, squinting and bobbing the way he does when he talks because he's lived alone for so long that the sound of his own words is like too-bright sunlight to him. "Can't not go now. Know whad ahm sayin? Am I righ?"

Albert stopped by one last time early yesterday in the course of his morning chores. "Nooo, bud ahh mean," he kept saying as I moved about the cabin, trying to decide what of Bex's she would want me to take. "Gonna go any day. Am I righ?" I took, in the end, only an old photo album that I'd found on the bookshelves and a tattered black notebook labeled "Wickerby Diary." The rest I left to go down with the ship.

It may have gone down already, though I've no way to tell. I could make a call—Wickerby does have a phone. But for all I know, the only thing left standing now is the door-post to which the phone's attached, and I'd be dialing a wide-open hilltop in Canada, the way people here in the city call empty sidewalk phone booths, let the rings dangle on the air.

I'll pick up the phone and dial the cold, rimless northern night. There'll be that cheap, crackling mimicry of distance in my ear. Then, around each ring, I'll begin trying to reassemble Wickerby, to rebuild the cabin in my mind, just as the man down on Lincoln Place in the house of refuse does all day, standing on the sidewalk amidst his belongings, his eyes closed, his hands patting up at the air, trying to mold it into walls.

Closing my eyes, I can see Wickerby now, can see the signs of the life I've just lived there—the plates, mugs and spices on the badly sloping shelves behind the sink, the eating utensils in the red metal tool kit on the center island chopping block. There's a giant, two-tiered woodstove, still standing, I'm certain, like a cast-iron altar at the very heart of the place. In the northwest corner, behind the exposed steps that lead to the sleeping loft, there's an oak table and chairs, and a paper kite hanging from an overhead support beam, and a canoe paddle nailed to the wall above the table, and a pair of snowshoes above a tall, mahogany secretary, its nooks and drawers filled with playing cards and dice and board games and fishing tackle. Most of the north wall is lined with bookshelves that frame a love seat, my favorite spot in the cabin, set right beneath the window with the plum tree branches bobbing outside it.

It still opens, that window. I imagine myself seated there again. Wickerby begins to coalesce around me, that feeling, almost painful, of a moment's passing there, and then it all comes apart, the cabin crumbling around its own tremulous mortar of twitched animal heads and wide-eyed stares, and the loud, waxen-winged scatter of a rooftop crow, like a broken fleck of night sky.

In the distant twilight, Manhattan is just a faint outline of gray, snuffable ash. The pigeons are still returning across the way, their bright underwings flashing above the rusted bronze eaves of the three-story walk-ups along Lincoln Place, people leaning, here and there, at their windowsills, the wide sky pressing down.

A woman steps now from a skylight door, her two German shepherds, brown and black, following behind her for their evening run. They go bounding across the stiled rooftops as though in some cloud-borne fox hunt, the tops of the back-alley ailanthus trees swaying on a soft wind behind them.

Directly below, people are hurrying along. They pass the man in the house of refuse, scatter briefly the stray cats that live just up the sidewalk from him atop a pile of old sofa cushions at the base of an abandoned brownstone. Everyone is heading to the far end of the block, where a street fair—The First Annual Washington Avenue Extravaganza—has been going since this morning.

I walked through it earlier today. Neighborhood kids were already lined up eight deep at the fair's only game booth, waiting for the chance to toss Ping-Pong balls into bowls of water and win a goldfish. There is also a ride, called the Top of the World, a red flatbed truck with a huge crescent-shaped metal cage on the back swung by two men. I can see just the tips of the crescent now, popping up briefly above the rooftops, children screaming, other children streaming along the sidewalk below, holding fistfuls of goldfish in clear plastic Baggies like upside-down animate bouquets.

Two starlings settle on the top railing of the fire escape just beside me. They preen, sing—antic, high-pitched clown-whistle sounds—then roll their heads to let the evening breeze comb their neck feathers. Wasps, listless, late-roused, summer-drunk drones, keep drifting in and out of my open window, their bodies bristling as they bob before the lighted TV screen, where a man holding a giant tape recorder explains that he's traveling the globe in hopes of capturing "the world's last noiseless dawns." He says he wants to preserve for posterity the increasingly rare sound of a sunrise without us, without any man-made noises.

From down the block, detached, muffled, beach-day screams keep drifting in off the Top of the World. I watch the fair-goers go up and down the avenue. Any minute, I keep thinking, Bex will phone. She'll fill me with stories of her travels, and then I'll tell her a story of my own, about my stay at her Wickerby. Or perhaps I'll say nothing about it, put it all down here instead in the Wickerby Diary for her to find later, with or without me—one last, sprawling entry into that ledger of impermanence.

Already I can sense it collapsing, not the cabin so much as the essence of the time that I've just spent there, the gradualness of a Wickerby day beginning to give way again to this one, where the eye pivots from one paved surface to the next through an endless juxtaposition of things we've made. It's a rich sensation, not a sad one. It's what, I now understand, I couldn't wait to come back here to feel.

I could have, with a few modifications to the cabin, easily stayed longer at Wickerby. I might even have lasted out a winter, staked my claim to the wreckage of Bex's past and then left her a message back here to come rejoin me in it. But the truth is that I couldn't stand it there any longer, not just the loneliness but the absence of all this around me tonight, this well-lit wreckage.

I could tell Bex tonight about the rare repose that

WICKERBY

I found at Wickerby and yet fully recognize and revel in only now that I'm back in the city, in the very place that will conspire to dispel the feeling. It's a feeling composed, I think, of little more than my repeated visits with blank hillsides and woods, places and silences which, nevertheless, the further I pursued them, the harder I listened there, the more they issued me the gentlest rebuke, disposed me, in the end, to want to leave, to return here to this home and begin longing again for the one I've just left behind.

I read recently about a man so rich he's built himself a log cabin on top of his Manhattan high-rise apartment building. Whenever he needs to get away from the city, he takes an elevator to the roof. He might be up there now, at his own set of north-wall bookshelves, at his own window with a tree, a potted tree, swaying outside. He might stay up there for as long as I did at Wickerby.

But when he takes the elevator back down, he won't feel this deep longing, won't see this city any differently. He won't see, as I suddenly do, the close alignment between Wickerby and here, as though the one inspired and informed the other, those blank hillsides giving rise to all these millions of lights—the rich man's high-rise cabin just one more among them—that I'll watch take hold here across the horizon tonight.

I'm putting it down now in the ledgers of impermanence, the story of my days at Wickerby, if only to prolong them, if only to stay awhile the spell of their passing.

DOWN ON LINCOLN PLACE, the man in the house of refuse stands on the sidewalk, patting at the air, trying to guard his home's wide corners against dissolution. He has just one piece of furniture, an old rattan sofa, cushionless, set against the closed steel shutter of an abandoned storefront. Two sections of wrought iron fence, bolstered by rows of cinder blocks, make up the house's side walls. A large black umbrella serves as a portable roof. At one end of the sofa, alongside a parked shopping cart, he has an elm sapling in a garbage can, the leaf-lined branches reaching back over into the area of his living room. At the sofa's opposite end, there's a gooseneck floor lamp rigged to a car battery. Behind the lamp is a New York City public telephone, its metal cord just long enough for him to be able to sit on his sofa when he's talking.

Often this past summer I'd stand in the field outside the cabin door, at the stretched end of Wickerby's telephone cord, having dialed this high-buildinged hubbub just to see if Bex had left me a message on our answering machine. My days were very empty there, and yet they seemed busy. Or they were, like the man in the house of refuse's days, very busy with their emptiness because the task never ends of having to embody, to internalize the whole outdoors.

He's always leaving, just as I would at Wickerby, going a short way off and then turning to look back, to regard his frail house from afar. He'll go half a block and then turn and look, as though trying to cement his place with prolonged stares. He'll go even farther, to the fire hydrant nearest Washington Avenue, collect some water in a bucket for washing and bring it back. Sometimes, he'll even venture to the corner of Washington, brush up against the passing fair crowd and then turn and saunter slowly home, somehow girding his place by the simple act of returning to it.

And yet no matter how diminished his house may be by this city pressing in all around it, he seems only encouraged by it and by the people passing everywhere up and down—emboldened enough by the daily commerce, in fact, that he can allow the very place that would consume him be his walls. At Wickerby, I had to suggest myself to every place and thing, narrate each of my movements lest they dissipate around me.

He's leaving again now, going to the hydrant with his bucket. He fills it, walks back and waters the elm sapling.

WICKERBY

It's the only tree left along Lincoln Place—that and a baby ailanthus sprouting from the base of a stairless, second-story doorway just beneath the broken windows of the pigeons' apartment. All the others disappeared during a mad tree-stealing spree that occurred here last spring just after Bex left for Africa. I don't know where or for how much one redeems a stolen tree in this city, but judging by the grounds around this building and all the sidewalk plots and postage stamp–sized yards of the neighborhood's apartment houses, people were making off with whatever sapling or shrub they could manage to uproot.

Our doorman started sitting outside each night with a baseball bat. Over at the Brooklyn Museum, the grounds-keeper took to chaining the trees down. One end of the chain he wrapped around the trunk, the other around a big rock that he'd bury a few feet into the ground. In the Brooklyn Botanic Gardens, twenty-four-hour security guards were put on patrol. One night while I was walking Lucy out front, a bright green Parks Department vehicle raced by with lights and sirens blaring, and a tree on its side in the back. That was when I began to think it might be a good time to get out of Brooklyn for a while.

The fact is that I had no intention of living in a crumbling log cabin five months ago, but then neither had I anticipated my life here coming apart the way that it did. It's kind of a tale of two ruins—one urban, the other remote; one fast-paced, one slow; one the result of too many people, the other of too few—and, as with any of these multistoried edifices surrounding me tonight, mine begins with a hole in the ground.

CHARLES SIEBERT

· · ·

The hole used to be my street, the one that runs in front of this apartment building, Eastern Parkway—"the world's first parkway," according to the sign just down the block on the lawn beside the Brooklyn Library and the Grand Army Plaza entrance to Prospect Park, where my street begins. A once-stately, six-lane thoroughfare bordered on either side by tree- and bench-lined promenades, the roadway was designed back in 1870 by the great landscape architects Frederick Law Olmsted and Calvert Vaux. They built parks all across this country, Central Park in Manhattan being their most famous, but Prospect Park was their self-proclaimed masterpiece: 526 sculpted acres of woods, water and glade which, bound as it is now on all sides by cement, is like some long, deep breath that they remembered to take for us within the shallow rigor of these streets.

My street was designed to be a kind of rolling extension of the park—thus the name "park-way"—and, according to accounts I've read, was originally supposed to connect with a whole series of new parks, thereby creating a vast system of what Olmsted called "greenbelts" that would, he thought, effectively break the city's ever-tightening choke hold of cement—an altogether grand scheme that came, however, to a rather abrupt and ignoble end about a mile and a half from here at what is now Ralph Avenue on the old eastern border of Brooklyn in the bombed-out ghetto of Brownsville.

Still, even in its much abridged and now time-worn version, the parkway does (when the city isn't digging

18

giant holes in it, that is) lend this area a certain air of civility and calm, like some extended bough of leafy grace to which I've often seen the most frazzled urban night-birds report, allowing their variously induced street buzzes to dissipate within the gentle abrasion of the passing cars.

A number of the giant elms originally chosen by Olmsted and Vaux for the precise blend of sunlight, shadow and breeze that elm branches bestow upon a pedestrian still line the promenades from end to end, each tree dedicated with a bronze plaque to a dead World War I soldier. City trees have to shoulder such burdens, the trade-off being that they often get better care. When the great epidemic of Dutch elm disease hit the U.S. in the 1940s, a good many of the specimens here were, unlike their rural counterparts, able to survive precisely because they had the likes of us so close by to attend to them.

As for the elms that did succumb, they were promptly replaced with silver maples, sycamores, pin oaks and black oaks, so that whatever brand of traffic we have concocted over the years—from horse-drawn carriages to electric trolleys to fly-by automobiles—there's long been a towering tunnel of interlocking tree limbs here to embrace and gently muffle the frenzied flow.

In fact, Eastern Parkway was one of the big reasons that I first decided to leave my too-cozy, sun-starved studio in Manhattan ten years ago and move out here to Brooklyn—move back, I should say, as I grew up in Brooklyn in the late 1950s, although in a different section of it, known as Flatlands, located just a couple of miles to the southeast alongside Marine Park and the Atlantic Ocean.

If you were to suddenly come upon my neighborhood the way I did ten years ago, exiting the subway at the Grand Army Plaza traffic circle and then walking up Eastern Parkway—as grand and as architecturally appointed as the Champs Elysees, right down to the plaza's slightly scaled-down model of the Arc de Triomphe, built to commemorate the Union Victory in the Civil War—then you'd probably think, as I did, that it's an ideal place to live.

From the plaza, walking eastward up a slight grade, you pass in close succession the Brooklyn Library, Botanic Gardens and Brooklyn Museum on your right, and, on your left, along the crest of an ancient glacial ridge, a steep, gently curving cliff-face of apartment buildings known in the 1920s as "The Gold Coast" for the legions of moneyed professionals who are said to have fought for living space here.

My building, situated diagonally across the parkway from the museum, is the last in this once-coveted row: a huge, redbrick, mock-Tudor affair known as Adelphi Hall. It features exposed wood trim, a gateway arch in front and a rather novel, if tortuous, multiwinged design that renders "Every Room . . . ," according to the original Realtor's advertisement, "an Outside Room!"—an early selling point which, in my case, however (sixth floor, rear), has come to mean a particularly good view of hell, or, at least, the bleak underbelly of Olmsted and Vaux's original pastoral vision: a burnt-out, bricked-up expanse of row houses and warehouses wherein people must daily make their way amidst the drug dealers, the overpriced supermarkets purveying mostly rancid goods and the multicolored-lightbulb-rimmed corner bodegas selling beer and pork rinds.

Mine is one of those once-great city neighborhoods the sad decline of which you'll often hear veteran New York City cab drivers and former residents of the area—mostly white, old-world immigrants who departed decades ago for the suburbs—lamenting. Of course, the fact that a similar lament is constantly being voiced by the neighborhood's current residents—mostly black and Hispanic Third World immigrants—seems to be lost upon almost everyone, certainly those who are supposed to be in a position to do something about it.

It's the kind of place to which public officials or official funds rarely come anymore. The schools are understaffed and poorly supplied. The stores are overpriced and poorly supplied. The neighborhood parks and playgrounds belong, by and large, to the dealers and doers. The police end all their foot patrols by dusk and come out at night only in squad cars, either to help clean up the dead dealers or to extort money from the live ones. The rest of us, meanwhile, just do our best to stay out of harm's way.

I'll never forget the summer night three years ago—it was just weeks before Bex had moved in with me—when our local Mr. Softee ice cream man was nearly killed down on Lincoln Place. I was sitting in this very room, at just about this hour, when I heard angry voices rising from the stoop of what, until it burned two years ago, had been the neighborhood crack house. By the time I'd gotten myself into the askance window position that one readily perfects here, the shooting had already begun. It had been going on for at least a minute when Mr. Softee, an apparent inebriate of his own repeating jingle, rolled right into the fray. He slammed on his brakes, then began backing madly up the street, his jingle, I swear, going into a wacky, high-pitched reverse with him.

After I'd managed to snap Lucy out of the whirling, four-claw nesting frenzy she immediately flies into on hearing any sudden loud noise (it looks like she's trying at once to fluff up and to fully merge with whatever it is she's lying on and has to date cost me three sets of sheets, a sofa and all of my car's upholstery), I saw my canary Rasteedy's perch vacantly swinging. I ran over to find her at the bottom of her cage, cowering in a yellow cloud of her own shed plumage.

Ever since, I've noticed more and more of my neighbors taking to the roofs for their walks and picnics. It used to be just the pigeon mumblers up here, chasing their flocks into the sky, but looking out toward Manhattan now, I can see people hunched around their barbecues, kids playing tar-roof soccer and basketball, others flying kites, the woman across the way still out running her dogs. It's like a whole other city trying to coalesce on the air.

Still, I don't mean to foster the impression one often gets from the local tabloids and nightly news reports about neighborhoods like mine that all is misery and danger here. The fact is that until the city came along last spring and dug that huge hole in my street, I had always found the conditions here to be quite livable. I have this spacious, relatively inexpensive, high-ceilinged, five-room apartment with its uninterrupted view (beyond the devastation) of the Manhattan skyline, just now beginning to harden again around a few scattered glints of window light. I have, as well (amidst the devastation), nearly all of Brooklyn's major cultural institutions within a brief stroll, including, on the far side of the Botanic Gardens, the Prospect Park Zoo. And I have, most important, always been able to find here some rendition, however compromised, of Olmsted and Vaux's original vision, a kind of urban-pastoral weave wherein appointed pavement keeps giving way to a provided pause.

To me this is a place where the very purpose of living in a city—which, unless I'm missing it entirely, has to do with the invigorating, if sometimes begrudging, proximity of my fellow humans and of our various pursuits within the cemented, high-storied context of that purpose—gets both underscored and gently undercut. Thus, on any given day here, you can step just down the parkway to the entrance of Prospect Park, pass through the granite portal of Endale Arch and, from all the fever and fuss, emerge suddenly out into the park's vast Long Meadow—"undulating," as Olmsted himself once described it, "without defined edges, its turf lost in a maze of the shadows of scattered trees."

It's a place where, after another string of seemingly pointless hours spent writing up here in the din-stoked ether, I can go across to the Prospect Park Zoo for an oddly restorative stare-down with their rhinoceros; or for a late-afternoon walk along the winding paths of the Japanese Garden, the shrubs there sculpted sideways, like drifting clouds, the same blue heron perched, motionless, atop the pond's NO FISHING sign, pinion of a passing day.

It's a place, finally, where, after that third or fourth volley of mid-afternoon gunfire has set off yet another discordant symphony of car alarms, I can always go across to the Brooklyn Museum's exhibit of nineteenth-century New York period rooms and, staring into the low-lit recesses of Colonel Robert Milligan's library, at least visit with the trappings of civility: the rosewood bookcases, gilded birdcages and stilled, dusty planets of shelved orreries; the little blond-haired boy-mannequin, sitting alone on the parquet floor, marching his long, circular line of toy animals, two by two, into the ark.

These do, at times, seem to me meager dividends for a tenure as long as mine here, myself now one of the true veterans of the neighborhood and its numerous affronts, not the least of these, in my case, being the requisite wariness about, and resentment of, my skin color.

I have, over the years, been seen by some as that first pale drop in a coming wave of gentrification, one which, despite a decade of rumors about its imminent approach, seems to be no closer. I've received, as well, countless nasty looks; have had cars chase me from crosswalks, and have, when I'm the driver, had pedestrians purposely slow down to strut that defiant, dare-you-to-drive-into-me strut across my front bumper. I have, finally, been told any number of times and in no uncertain terms (although always to my back, just after I've walked by) to get the fuck out, an option that I most likely would have exercised by now if not for the somewhat embarrassing fact that as a very sporadic wage earner, I long ago became unduly dependent upon the good graces of a landlord who has consistently allowed me to be three months late with the rent.

In the meantime, I've watched nearly the entire population of this building turn over at least once, which tells me I'm not the only genius who's recognized the desirability of moving somewhere with, let's say, fewer stray bullets in the air, the basic premise being that among the myriad ways there are in this world to permanently exit it, interrupting an errant discharge from a drug dealer's dispute has got to be about the stupidest.

Still, in the course of my days here, while waiting for my station to improve, or for my "day" to "come," as Jimmy, the Jamaican painter of our building's vacated apartments, always puts it to me whenever I bump into him in the hallway—"You still here?" he says. "Don't worry. Your day will come."—I have, if only by default, learned a few significant lessons.

It's not, for example, until you've lived in a place like this for a while that you realize just how much safety, how much plain old static normalcy there is at the heart of a so-called trouble spot. Days unfold here as they do all over the city, with the early-morning clamor of metal store shutters and that high-whining wail, elephantine, of the sanitation trucks.

People rush out to move their cars to the legal side of

the street just ahead of the parking cops. The mumblers are chasing their flocks into the sky. The pigeons across from me are already out foraging, shifting with the random street noises back and forth from eave to building eave, as those two shepherds go bounding across the opposing rooftops, their owner lagging behind, naked beneath her breeze-blown, yellow bathrobe, drifting sleepily about the skylight.

Directly below, the man in the house of refuse folds his bedding neatly beneath the rattan sofa. He tends to the cats next door, set cans of food down into their cushioned square, pours them milk from a carton, cats swirling up, over and down his arms. Then he sweeps the sidewalk. He sweeps inward toward the center of his house as one would the dirt on the kitchen floor, and then, where the border of his belongings ends, he sweeps outward, toward the curb, cleaning up the yard around his house. On Mondays, Wednesdays and Fridays, he waits for the city street-sweeper to come by and then follows behind it, sweeping.

At nine A.M., St. Theresa de Avila's twin church-tower bells toll, and in the wide, ensuing silence, you can often hear the children singing their morning songs over at the Nile Day-Care Center on Washington Avenue. Across the avenue, J, Mr. J, Mr. Joseph P. Lawson, owner of Mr. J's Variety Store, where I buy my newspaper every morning, runs out of newspapers by about ten A.M. (he says they never deliver him enough) and then, as acting president of the Washington Avenue Merchants' Association (such as it is), he locks his store up for the rest of the morning and takes his daily stroll up and down the avenue, checking in with his fellow merchants.

There's the extended group of brothers and cousins from Yemen who run the C-Town supermarket, where even the lightbulbs and laundry detergent have gone bad. Right beside them is Rose, longtime owner of Rose's Liquors. A holdout from the old neighborhood, she seems to think of me as a little atoll in the surrounding sea of darkness. She calls me "dearie," goes on for hours about the area's decline and her plans to leave it, and invites me in behind her bullet-proof glass to get the bottles that she can't reach. The proprietors of Chez La Mi Tio Tio Restaurant, on the other hand, always look askance when I enter. They ask me pointedly, each time I order it, if I really do like roti.

There's Mr. and Mrs. Peterson, the elderly black couple who own Peterson's Dry Cleaners. Tom, a Lithuanian immigrant, runs Tom's Luncheonette, a fixture in the neighborhood since the 1930s and the only place for miles to eat a real, sit-down breakfast. And then, of course, there's Gerry, the owner of Mayday Hardware, another holdover from the early days. My guess is he inherited the store from his father. Pudgy, flush-cheeked, hyperactive, deeply insecure Gerry in his round-toed, rubber-soled shoes, and plastic, shirt-pocket pen pouch, who can transform the purchase of a simple screw into such an elaborate display of his knowledge and proficiency that you'll go miles the next time to buy that screw elsewhere; Gerry, the previous president of the Merchants' Association, who continually drives

J to distraction with advice and complaints about the neighborhood.

J's own business pivots mostly around newspaper and candy sales, although, it being a "variety store," he also features a wide assortment of odds and ends, from batteries to minor hardware to greeting cards to women's hairpieces, all of it crammed into a space no bigger than a walk-in closet. You can make a five-cent photocopy there or, sitting along a narrow back counter opposite shelves of school supplies and portable TVs and tape cassette players, have a cup of coffee and an egg sandwich prepared by J.

On the wall behind the counter, there's an open *Playbill* from the early 1970s with a picture of J—tall, broad-shouldered, bearlike—as the lead in an all-black repertory company's off-off-Broadway production of *Othello*. The show ran for a couple of weeks, J says, after which he gave up acting. He tried briefly to revive the air-conditioning repair business he'd started upon his discharge from the army, and then he abandoned that scheme and bought the variety store. He opened on that infamous steamy summer night in 1977 when all the lights went out along the eastern seaboard, and he was forced to sit up until morning at his candy counter, guarding his place with a loaded shotgun as almost every other store along Washington Avenue got looted out of business, and a good portion of the neighborhood went up in flames.

Ever since, J has acted as the area's unofficial mayor, this ruin's caretaker as Albert is Wickerby's—although I'd say J contributes far more to the long-term prospects of his wardenry than Albert does to his. He's forever wandering up and down Washington Avenue, dreaming of new businesses for the vacant lots, and doing his best to steer local kids clear of drugs and of the neighborhood gangs that roam the broken-down streets off behind Lincoln Place, their eerie, whooping signal calls—exactly like those of the humpback whales—echoing on the night air.

He spends hours in the tiny office behind his breakfast counter, writing or phoning representatives of area banks to petition them for small-business loans on behalf of prospective merchants. He even got the man in the house of refuse started by securing for him the shopping cart with which he collects his ad hoc furnishings. On Sundays, J leads the local Baptist church congregation in hymns.

When he finally secured his own loan last spring, J built himself a new front display window and a self-draining ice-tub, which he was planning to set out on a sidewalk stand and fill with cold drinks. "They should really be popular with the kids in the summer months," he told me. A portion of his loan he put toward organizing today's Extravaganza, all of it his doing. He handed me a flier last spring, the morning I left for Wickerby. I still have it here on the coffee table, the long list of neighborhood musicians, including Gunja Man, Wicky Wacky, Wainsy Ranks, Mikey Merican, Shiny Culture and Poets of Tomorrow.

When St. Theresa de Avila's bells toll again at six P.M., J and his fellow merchants—all except for the corner bodegas—have closed up shop. The Mr. Softee ice cream truck has already made a number of passes. At dusk, the mumblers' pigeons are coming in, as are the ones across the way. The cars have resettled into their nightly spaces, and all around me the same constellation comes forward again in the deepening darkness of passing lives and flickering TV sets.

In fact, I would say the real news about this neighborhood—though it rarely qualifies as such—is how infrequent the mad outbursts really are; how dignified and courageous most people remain in difficult circumstances. Mostly, as I say, people just live here, in these apartments, on these blocks. I pass my neighbors every day. We exchange the usual cursory greetings, talk about the weather, complain about the building's squeaky elevators or the car alarm that kept us up most of the night.

Sometimes we have tenants' meetings downstairs in the lobby and voice our complaints about the building together: the doorman sleeping at night, and the broken intercoms, and the need for outdoor spotlights to expose Adelphi Hall's many dark, thief-filled nooks. We complain about the neighborhood, and these days, because it's been on everyone's mind here—and caked onto the bottom of our shoes, and drawn in endless muddy rivulets through the downstairs lobby, and the elevators, and into our apartments—we complain about that huge hole in our street.

Every other month, J organizes a neighborhood meeting over at the Nile Day-Care Center. He invites in local police chiefs or politicians. They profess their concern, make promises, and then they just stand there, nervously shifting back and forth, as everyone complains about the need for more patrolmen, and better services, and more representation, and, these days, about the need for a goddamned street.

IT WAS EARLY LAST APRIL—just days after Bex left for Africa, on what has now become a nearly six-month journey to write a magazine story about a film crew that's following one of the world's last nomadic tribes, the Turkana, around northern Kenya—that a city-hired construction company arrived here and dug the hole in our parkway. This would not have been such a big deal except for the fact that the very same construction company had only recently filled in that hole, one they'd originally dug three years earlier at the beginning of what the newspapers were then claiming would be a two-year project to restore Eastern Parkway to its former grandeur and elegance.

Mr. J has been telling me for years that he sees no reason why this neighborhood, with its prime location and obvious cultural attributes, can't be revitalized, which is why he more than anyone else was thrilled at the sight of that hole in the ground when it first got dug three years ago. It was J, in fact, who first told me of the parkway reconstruction project, information he'd received in his dealings with city officials. He talked about the new sewer pipes and road surface and cobblestone promenades, everything down to the planned installation of faux-Victorian, gas lamp–shaped streetlights, and new bronze World War I commemorative plaques to replace all the ones that have, over the years, been pried up and sold to scrap dealers. And he talked about all the elm saplings that would be planted in order to fill in, over time, the gaps in the bower of trees above.

Ours is clearly the sort of neighborhood with problems far deeper than the restoration of some sun-dappled elm shade could ever resolve. J, for one, has been saying from the start that he thinks the money would have been far better spent on things like computers for the area schools or the building of playgrounds where kids could throw a basketball through something more lasting and resonant than a plastic milk crate lashed to a fence.

Still, the feeling was that any refurbishment would be welcome, any attention from an outside authority, and once the digging began, you could sense the general mood of the neighborhood improving, if only at the prospect of officially sanctioned destruction, which, for a brief time at least, seemed to bring to a halt the haphazard, criminal variety that typically reigns.

I remember the day the crew arrived, it being the very day that Bex moved in with me here three years ago. I'd gone outside, as I do every morning, to walk Lucy and buy the newspapers at J's. There on the parkway's eastern horizon was the earthmover, its huge, extended claw pulling up sections of street surface like a finger dragged through stale cake icing.

Every morning afterward for months, it seemed, another layer of parkway was being unearthed and lifted out into bold relief against the sky: old street surfaces, trolley tracks, water mains and sewer pipes. Where the digging finally stopped right out front at the corner of Eastern Parkway and Washington Avenue, the hole expanded to encompass what looked to be Brooklyn's main infrastructural intersection, the Times Square of sewerage, with bulbous joints and pressure gauge wheels worthy of great steamships, and fist-sized bolts that two workers would have to hold on to each other to turn. Then, day after day, piece by piece, that whole assemblage would be excavated and carted away. It was like being on hand for the dismantling of recent history.

Before long, there was a twelve-foot-deep, street-wide trench running the entire two-mile length of the parkway, with thick wooden planks set in to reinforce the steep mud sides. The hole seemed to delight everyone, to imbue the neighborhood with the giddy air of a school snow day. Often you'd see people walking up to the edges just to stare in. There's something deeply diverting, satisfying, about a big hole in the ground, especially in a city where it's so easy to forget the ground; where you can get so caught up in this one fast, paved, sky-scraped version of a day that you forget there are other days elapsing slowly elsewhere and sideways.

Children, I've thought, are so drawn to digging and all of its accoutrements—the dump trucks, tractors and earth-movers—because they've spent so little time on the earth that perhaps delving into it seems to them like a way back home. But we never really lose that feeling, no matter how frayed and frenzied our lives get; never lose that urge to stop and peer in through the plywood borders around an inner-city construction site. There's a nearly primeval surprise and permission to pause we feel at the sight of the earth again, a sudden hole in the seemingly impregnable argument for ourselves that is a city. No one ever bothers with the sign that explains what's going to be built next. We seem to revel more in the interruption of what we've already made, just stand there staring into dirt as though trying to recall something, a lost phrase, the thread of a different argument, of an uninflected earth.

All that was left of our particular block of the parkway was the lone, exposed stem of the two-beat-clanking manhole cover that passing cars used to play. On warm summer and early fall evenings, Bex and I would sit out under the parkway trees atop the cool, terra-cotta replacement sewer pipes, stacked there beside the hole. Just behind us would be the giant earthmover, always left out overnight, unlocked and unattended, too big even for this neighborhood's tireless thieves to take, the mover's claw resting in the same position: turned back inward toward the glass control cabin and palm up, its five dinosaur-sized, oddly delicate digits pressed flush against the earth.

For a time, all traffic was diverted elsewhere, and as you looked out through the trees across the parkway's hollowed-out lanes, it was as though the city itself had been undone, the entire machine muffled and seized the way it is in the hours just after a snowstorm. At night, hundreds of bats swooped through the spot-lit haze above the Brooklyn Museum's center dome, and all around the heads of the life-sized granite statues along the frieze: Confucius, Mohammed, Moses, Aristotle, Plato and so on. All the great seers and thinkers of history, standing up there, clutching their scrolls, staring down upon my now quiescent neighborhood as though suddenly taken with the possibility of suggesting something different.

They might at least have recommended the name of a new construction company. Bex and I sensed early on that we'd be getting more than a passing glimpse of the earth here just from the way the workers were going about their job. There was a certain lack of urgency in their movements: guys walking back and forth nowhere slowly with arm's-length wrenches, listlessly bouncing pickaxes off curbsides before heading over to the aluminum-paneled coffee wagon.

And even then, long after others had begun to lose patience with the inconvenience of having no street, I remained untroubled by it. Perhaps because I don't have a job that requires daily commutes or any hurried immersion in street commerce, I continued to delight in the diversion, found myself reveling if only in the weightiness of the construction crew's time-wasting. Somehow their day seemed the perfect antidote to mine: sitting for hours up here in the windowed air, drinking too much coffee, my body growing ever lighter with abstraction so that by day's end I'm like a smiley-faced helium balloon, bobbing against the ceiling.

Still, a city neighborhood can go for only so long without a street before the whole proposition of a city gets called into question. Months would pass sometimes when the workers didn't show. Then, well over a year into the project, they just stopped coming altogether. Night after night, the hole filled with garbage and rainwater, the parkway's trees looming above it in some dreary pantomime of a wooded riverbank. Our mock-Tudor apartment house soon resembled a moated castle, a few wood planks leading from our front entrance serving as the drawbridge, and only an exposed umbilical of telephone cables, sagging above the hole, tethering us to the outside world.

We tend to live braced for bad news here, be it the nightly report of pistols or the newspaper story that appeared around the time the parkway reconstruction crew first stopped coming, the story explaining that our entire local police precinct was being relocated for complicity in the neighborhood drug trade, cops shaking down dealers and reselling their drugs. This was hardly news to me, as I'd been watching patrol cars for years roll, sans flashing lights or sirens, to slow stops in the wee hours before the stoop of the old crack house and then roll quietly off again.

Thus, when city officials revealed near the end of the project's second year that the construction company they'd hired had, amidst charges of mafia corruption and continued mismanagement of their other contracts, gone bankrupt, no one here even blinked. Neither were we particularly ruffled by the announcement some three months later that the city had finally decided to bail out said construction company because, after much deliberation, it was determined that it would cost the city a lot more to go through the process of hiring a new one.

All anyone here cared about was that by late last summer, work had finally resumed, and with such renewed vigor that by December, the hole was filled in, a new road surface laid, and a number of the young elm saplings planted. A bitter February and early March brought work to a halt again, but with the arrival of spring, the mood here was as bright as I've ever seen it.

A city wears the changing seasons with more ardor than the country: the isolate blossoms, the thin sweetness of thawing cement, the air retaining, like a late-afternoon lake, its inner pockets of chill. Over at the gardens, the star magnolias and weeping Higan cherries had begun to bloom, while up and down the streets the languid, loose-boned melody of ice cream trucks could be heard again on the evening air. On sunny days, I'd set Rasteedy's cage out on the windowsill. She'd swing there in her webbed square of sky, watching the pigeons across the way, sometimes engaging in offbeat duets with the fire-escape starlings or with the wood doves that nest here in the eaves, Rasteedy climbing the frail latticework of her own birdsong into an ecstatic, nearly inaudible register of trilling that seemed to transport her right out of herself.

By April, I was reveling in the parkway's apparent renaissance, allowing myself to imagine the new gas lamps and mall benches and the fully restored whir of an unimpeded traffic flow. Then, early one mid-April morning, a week or so after Bex had left for Africa, I went outside with Lucy to get the papers at Mr. J's and saw, just as I had three years earlier, that giant earthmover out on the eastern horizon, tearing the whole place up again, "an apparent flaw" the next day's newspapers explained, "in the replacement sewer pipes."

Somehow the coincidence of Bex's departure and the hole's untimely return, in conjunction with all the other frustration and anger that tends to accrue in a place where city money is spent on a road rather than on the people who live beside it, set off a downward spiral of events that would ultimately catch the attention even of a devoted, some might say sense-deadened, city-dweller like myself.

An early heat spell set in, days so hot the evening moon was coming up dull orange like slag from a blast furnace. Lucy had taken to sleeping on the bathroom tiles, her face stuck in a winded pant, while downstairs on Lincoln Place even the all-night stoop-dwellers were deserting their street buzz for the drone of air conditioning. It got so quiet here at night that as I lay in bed I could identify the far-off gunshots like bird calls in the woods at Wickerby: the faint balloon bursts of the .22, the deliberate, driving pops of a .38, the rapid tappings of the nine-millimeter machine-gun pistol, or "street-sweeper," as it's commonly known here.

In the *Stanstead Journal,* the newspaper I bought this summer in the tiny village of Georgeville, just a few miles down the road from Wickerby, there was a small box for bird watchers, noting which species had been spotted and where. Here, the newspapers were running a box for shootings, a feature in which my precinct began to figure a bit too prominently last spring.

Over in the projects at the north end of Washington Avenue where the old Ebbets Field used to be, two women were wounded on the same night while standing at their kitchen windows doing dishes; wounded, it was later determined, by target-practice bullets, kids shooting between the high rises, their target, they were quoted as saying, being the sky. A week later, our neighborhood nightclub, Love People II, located at the base of the Ebbets Field projects, just across from the Prospect Park Zoo, was closed down after a *Time* magazine article on drugs and inner-city violence cited the place as one of the top homicide spots in the country, averaging a murder a week.

I had, by this point, truly begun to wonder if the construction crew hadn't dug too deep the second time around, upsetting, perhaps, one of the Egyptian tombs stored in the vast subterranean coffers of the Brooklyn Museum, thereby unleashing some ancient curse upon this neighborhood. It seemed as good an explanation as any for the goings-on here last spring: the preternaturally early heat spell, the sudden, mad tree-stealing spree, the sharply rising number of stray bullets, and all the lopped-off Santeria rooster heads in Mt. Prospect Park, a tree-rimmed hilltop alongside the Brooklyn Museum where I often run with Lucy in the late afternoon.

And then there was that one particularly hot night when a couple of neighborhood kids sneaked into the zoo after closing and took a swim in the polar bears' moat. I heard the distant gunfire at about eight-thirty P.M., but that being nothing unusual here, it wasn't until I got the newspaper the following morning at J's that I learned what had happened: how the police, responding to a call about screams coming from the zoo, arrived to find the bears pawing at the limp body of the boy who didn't make it back out in time. On the off chance that he was still alive, or that the other boy might be hiding somewhere in the lair, the cops blew away the bears with shotguns.

Shortly thereafter, the zoo was closed for renovations. Most of the large animals, according to the woman who answered my phone call at the zoo's administrative offices, were being permanently relocated to other, more spacious facilities around the country.

"And the rhinoceros?" I asked.

"You mean Rudy," she said. "He's leaving tomorrow for a better life in Michigan."

A FEW DAYS AFTER RUDY had left for Michigan, two weeks after Bex's departure for Africa, I decided to set out for Wickerby. I didn't have many other getaway options, what with Lucy, Rasteedy and very limited funds. In fact, I had only Wickerby, or, I should say, the memory of it from my one visit.

Based upon what Bex had told me about the place, I was fairly certain that if it was still standing, no one would be living there. Bex's parents and an aunt and uncle originally bought the cabin and the surrounding 150 acres of woods for a grand total of six thousand dollars back in 1963, when Bex was just three years old, growing up in Montreal. She and her sisters and cousins spent all of their childhood summers and school holidays at the cabin. But somehow after Bex's parents divorced, and the children got older and went their separate ways, everyone just stopped going to Wickerby.

Bex says that her mother named the place after the wicopy, a native shrub also known as the leatherwood, which has small yellow flowers and a tough, pliable bark that the Indians are said to have once used for lashings and early settlers for carriage reins. "Wickerby," I'm told, is supposed to suggest the stately English country manor that Bex's mother, who grew up poor in London's East End, could never afford, although when I first heard Bex say the word, I pictured nothing habitable. It sounded more like some obscure British lawn game, or the most delicate basket, a frail weaving of bramble and air, an image which I thought pretty much suited the actual place that first time I'd set eyes on it six summers ago.

We stayed only a few weeks that visit and hardly made an impression upon it—on the dust and the depth of Bex's memories, on the awful weight of each day's passing. We talked often afterward about going back and really establishing ourselves there, but somehow never found the time. It takes time, I know now, more than I'll ever have, to truly arrive at a place like Wickerby.

Under W in an old address book lying here in Bex's top dresser drawer, I found the combination to the cabin's front-door lock. I threw clothes in one duffel bag, tossed books in another, packed the pet food and the birdcage, got a special bird travel box for Rasteedy, and drugged Lucy with a horse dose of Dramamine.

WICKERBY

I had no way to contact Bex and tell her of my sudden change of plans. The last correspondence I'd received from her was a postcard, dated April 2, Nairobi: an aerial photo of thousands of flamingos flocking over Lake Nakuru like a spill of pink paint across a black tile floor.

"My sweet pea," it begins. "Pea still on the vine, perfect pea," and then proceeds to explain that the expedition has been stalled somewhere outside Nairobi due to a protracted squabble with Kenyan officials over whether the tribeswomen will be filmed bare-breasted, which the crew, striving for utter authenticity, preferred, or clothed, which the government, not wanting their people to appear too primitive, was insisting on.

Bex then goes on to describe, in maddening detail, her elation over having learned to drive the film crew's twenty-ton equipment truck through the gnarled streets of downtown Nairobi, a hasty postscript mentioning that it could be months before they resolved the "breast matter" and got the necessary permits to proceed further.

I knew then that I wouldn't be hearing from Bex for some time, but, on the off chance that the nomads would be leading her past one of those rare Rift Valley phone booths, I decided to leave her a message here on the answering machine. "I've gone to Wix," was all it said. Bex has always called it Wix.

My trip did not have the most auspicious beginning. To facilitate loading the car, I'd parked it the night before in a space directly in front of our building, having taken care, as well, to leave it on the legal side of the re-dug park-way—because while the city has been in no particular hurry to give us our street back, it's been downright vigi-lant about enforcing alternate-side-of-the-hole parking regulations.

I gathered all my belongings in the lobby and then went outside to find that the car was gone. In any other cir-cumstance this would not have been such an upsetting development. If you've never owned a car in New York City—have never dealt with the day-long searches for a parking space, or waits on line to pay for an unjustified parking violation; have never engaged in the ongoing bat-tle against theft that has people here installing steering wheel locks out of medieval torture chambers, and ten-melody car alarms, and absurd signs in their windshields detailing all the things that there are not in the car to steal—then you might not understand how liberating the thought of having the entire burden lifted from you can be.

In this particular instance, however, I was finally ready to get out of here and had just lost my only means of doing so. Then I stepped up closer to the parkway. A mud slide, it seems, triggered by an overnight downpour, had deposited my car, passenger side first, into the puddle of muddy water at the base of the newly redug hole.

For the longest time, I just stood there, staring down at it. The construction crew was on the job bright and early that morning, pulling up sections of flawed sewer pipe at the far end of the block. One of the workers—the foreman, I think—did eventually notice me. He walked over with his cup of coffee in one hand and a cigarette in the other.

"Is that your car?"

I nodded. He turned—a shag of silver-gray hair jutting through the back arch of his cap—put his coffee cup in the same hand as the cigarette, and gave a piercing, two-fingered whistle toward the man up in the earthmover's glass control cabin. Within moments, the claw was sweeping toward us, breaking off a number of elm sapling branches before swaying to a stop directly above the hole.

Then the foreman—for reasons I still can't fathom—told me to get in my car, and I obeyed. Holding on to the edge of the hole, I hopped down onto the car's upturned side. I then knelt over the driver's-side door, opened it like a submarine hatch and, with the support of the seat-belt shoulder harness, slipped down into the driver's seat and strapped myself in.

I sat there, staring out sideways through the windshield as though stuck on a steep bank turn. It was very dark. I felt faint tendrils of earth-chill. Directly above me, there was only a thin tracery of tree branches against the morning sky, and the tiny silhouette of the foreman's hand gesturing at a gathering eclipse of earthmover claw.

I watched it drop to within a few feet of my car, and then the foreman was down in the hole with me, attaching Y-shaped cables from the claw to my front and back bumpers. He climbed back out. There was a loud engine thrust. The cables went taut. My car snapped upright and level with the earth. Then, with a second thrust, I was airborne, dangling above the topmost branches of the parkway's trees.

I was now, however briefly, eye to eye with Plato,

Aristotle, Confucius and the rest. Dangling there, steering, pointlessly, into the breeze, I could see as I imagine Olmsted and Vaux once did, with a nearly sense-splitting attention to both appointed detail and dreamy overview. Eastern Parkway was just a thin tributary of green winding down into Prospect Park's wide woods, where a feathery patina of new spring leaves covered acres of bare-branched bronchia. Then I looked down, peered again into the black depths of that hole into which I'd been staring for so many years, and suddenly, I could hear it—the lost phrase, the thread of that other argument, of that slowly elapsing, sideways day that is Wickerby.

There was another loud engine thrust, and then everything blurred as the claw swung out from the hole and set me back down on an intact section of parkway. The foreman came around, unhooked the cables, knocked twice on my hood.

"Okay," he said. "You're on your own."

I left about midday, the car's passenger-side doors still dripping muddy water as I stopped off at J's, bought the newspapers and a coffee to go, and then headed north up Washington Avenue onto the elevated lanes of the Brooklyn-Queens Expressway, Lucy in the back with the luggage, Rasteedy up front in the perforated bird travel box, which fit flush within the dashboard ashtray.

It was a clear, cool day, the previous night's storm having ushered in new air, and on either side of the expressway, above Williamsburg's and Greenpoint's dark, tumbledown expanse of skylights and factory smokestacks, the pigeon mumblers were out on their roofs, chasing their flocks with long poles into the sky, urging them to fly farther away for the simple thrill of watching what they love leave.

I knew a mumbler once, some fifteen summers ago. I was subletting an apartment in Greenpoint, a top-floor place (I seem to be drawn to them) so close to the expressway that I could study the faces in the rush-hour traffic. The mumbler had the apartment directly across the expressway from mine. One afternoon, I saw him climb out through a trapdoor in his roof. He walked over to his coop—a long rectangular structure with its own flat tar roof on top. It looked like a house adrift atop a larger house. He propped open the coop's wide front window slat and waited there as, one by one, and then in hurried bunches, pigeons appeared, alighting briefly, then dropping down to the tar roof below.

They weren't the sooted slate-gray of the everyday pigeons that live across from me, the kind mumblers call "mutts" or "street rats." These were white, red, cream and calico, select breeds with names like Russian High Flyers and West of Englands, each with its own distinctive flying style: the tumblers and rollers and tiplers. Hundreds had gathered there at the mumbler's feet. He seemed to wade through them toward the back of the roof, tossing down handfuls of seed from an old coffee can. He put the can down on the roof's back retaining wall, then picked up a long pole with a flag attached, sounded a sharp, loud whistle, and sent the whole flock skyward.

They went up as one, pulling higher in tight spirals,

their white underwings refracting the sunlight all at once as they turned, like sudden wind over a sidewalk puddle. They climbed straight up and then seemed to catch the wind and ride it sideways and east, out past the verdigris bell towers of St. Ignatius cathedral, past the red-checkered water tanks of Maspeth, Queens, toward Middle Village and Forest Hills, where the flock became just a slow-blinking dot against a distant cloud.

Every afternoon that mumbler would send up his flock, and then he'd wait for its return. Much of the time he'd be in a little wooden shanty at the back of the roof. It was just high enough to stand in and had windows on all four sides like a ship's pilot house. He'd spend hours up there, the shanty's pale light ripening in the gathering dusk, the mumbler idling about inside, tuning his radio, boiling water on a hot plate, reading the paper, occasionally combing the horizon with his binoculars.

The man's entire life seemed to be conducted between his apartment and his rooftop. One evening, I saw him on the roof with a woman. He flagged his pigeons into the sky, and as they turned tight circles above, he made love to her in a chair beside the shanty. It was as if he'd perfected a way of leaving the city without actually having to; as if he'd achieved the next stage in the evolution of the urban dweller: to have gone from living on a fully paved-over earth to never having to alight there at all.

I did finally bump into him on the ground one evening, in the delicatessen at the base of my Greenpoint apartment building. We started talking about pigeons, and then he invited me up to his roof. After chasing his birds, he looked across the horizon and pointed out all the other mumblers to me—"mumblers," he explained, because they spend so much time on the roof with their pigeons, they start to sound like them. He'd point to each of the flocks in the sky and then draw an imaginary line down from the birds to the silhouette of a man looking up at them from the roof below and say, "That's Gus, and that's Rocky, and there's Spike, and Crazy Coonie, and Frankie High Loft. . . ." I could see the slipshod, stunted skyline of all their coops and shanties, another city above the actual one; a place that begins where the concrete ends and is composed of little else but shifting flocks of tossed-off cares.

Sometimes, the mumbler told me, birds don't come back. Other mumblers often capture them. It's all part of the game. One mumbler sees another's birds going by and sends his flock up to "mix" with them. One flock tries to knock the other out of its flying pattern and assume the strays into its own. I've seen these exchanges here above the roofs of Crown Heights, like mid-air privateering expeditions, street fights without weapons, without streets, a disembodied clash of winged wills. A flock might come back either shy some pigeons or sporting a few new ones. Captives are usually brought to local pet shops and exchanged for a bag of pigeon feed. Mumblers can go and buy back their caught birds, but it's more or less a point of honor and pride among mumblers not to.

I was taken one evening down to the local pigeon shop in Williamsburg. PAT'S PETS, read the faded sign above the door on the corner of a dank, factory-lined street just a few blocks over from the East River. It looked like no pet store I'd ever seen: no puppies tumbling in the front-window wood shavings; no tropical fish tanks; no perch birds asleep on themselves—just brown paper lining an empty display window.

Inside, the shop was bare but for a cracked glass cashier counter, a couple of metal leashes hanging from hooks, and some faded boxes of Hartz Mountain canary food on a shelf. Mumblers were everywhere, sitting on folding chairs and sacks of pigeon feed, including a good many of the mumblers who had been pointed out to me from the roof days before. They had big, weathered, seaman's faces, guys from all over Brooklyn and Queens connected to one another merely by the flight of their birds.

At the back of the shop, through a swinging brown door with a round porthole window in it, there was a brashly lit, room-sized birdcage. The walls were lined from floor to ceiling with narrow white shelves. Hundreds of brightly colored pigeons were perched along them, wide-eyed and tremulous, a roomful of uneasy, earthbound spirits.

All night the mumblers told mumbling stories. One guy had a heart attack on his roof and nearly died because he refused to come down until his birds were back. Another mumbler's wife recently left him because he spent too much time on the roof and wouldn't even agree to have a phone installed in his shanty.

"That's exactly the kind of thing I go to the roof to get away from," he shouted.

One of the younger mumblers in the shop that night

had just gotten married the week before. One of his mumbler buddies arrived at the ceremony with a scaled-down, plywood replica of the actual wedding chapel in the back of his station wagon. When the ceremony was over and everyone was throwing rice, he opened the mini-chapel doors and let fly a flock of the purest white tiplets anyone had ever seen.

I checked, as I always do when I'm driving the expressway, for that mumbler's roof on my way to Wickerby last spring. He wasn't up there, but I could see his coop, remodeled now, the top of it painted a bright orange, probably to make it easier for his birds to spot on their way back in. The same shanty stood at the back of the roof, fifteen winters worse for the wear but, just as I'd find Wickerby, still upright, still habitable.

Whenever his flock came back that summer in Greenpoint, they'd hover above the roof and slap the tips of their wings together the way the ones in the apartment across from me do when they're coming in. Pigeons, the mumbler told me, get excited when they see home. They'd hold there in the sky above him until he let loose with one of his whistles, and then the whole flock would spill down like water from a pitcher. Spreading more handfuls of seed, he'd usher them all back into the coop. Then he'd lock up the shanty, walk over to the shaft of light shining up through the roof's open trapdoor and slip down into it, two hands reaching up again to pull the hatch over and repair the darkness.

Moments later, I'd see him again at his apartment window, arms crossed on the sill in the same white T-shirt, sleeveless. He'd lean, slightly, look out past the expressway and the tumbledown rooftops of Greenpoint, over the East River to Manhattan. He'd look as though he didn't quite recognize the place, as though, like me tonight, he'd just returned from a long time away and this city seemed both foreign to him and entirely natural, a deeply shameless play of lights: the slow slide and blink of passing river barges and landing jets; the unsprocketed flicker of subways through bridge trellises; the expressway traffic's long-snaking lava streams, red and white; and, along the darkening, factory-lined streets directly below our windows, the lone, wobbly headlights of the heavy flatbed trucks that would rumble by each evening toward the East River junkyards, carrying loads of scrap metal, the gathered dross of another day's smelting.

Were I a mumbler, I thought as my car climbed the Kosciusko Bridge above Newton, Maspeth and Whale Creek, all clogged with barges; above the grave-studded knolls of Calvary Cemetery, rolling to the sheer, living monuments of Manhattan in the distance; were I a mumbler, I could have my life here and leave it, too. As it was, I had all my cares with me, and seven more hours of driving to get to my own rooftop shanty far above the streets.

ONE DISTINCT ADVANTAGE of making a sudden departure like mine is that it allows you to get away from your life without waking it up. Then, if you've gotten enough of a head start, you can look back and at least begin to discern the vague outlines of something before it all catches up with you and overwhelms you again.

In truth, I didn't see much beyond the luggage—the plain, unalterable testimony of my belongings: two canvas duffel bags, one of clothes, one of books; a black shoulder satchel of writing notebooks and pens; a portable radio/cassette player; an electric coffeemaker; two half-gallon jugs of bourbon; and a folded birdcage. It seemed, if nothing else, an enviably unfettered existence: myself, a dog, a canary and a far-flung near-wife. Bex says that I should just call her my wife, but I think we should get married first, and she'd rather not, as she's tried that once already and failed.

The first few hours of the trip flew past, fueled by the sheer thrill of escaping Brooklyn. Still, the reality of having to resume my life in a place that I wasn't even sure existed any longer, or that I could even find without Bex, soon had me easing up a bit on the accelerator. In fact, the closer I drew to Wickerby that day, the more I found myself hoping that my fears about its collapse would be borne out, that I would crest the top of the entrance road and see just a heap of logs or an empty field, Albert having chopped the place up and added it to the long row of firewood he keeps along his back pasture fence. I'd spend a few nights at one of the lakeside inns in Georgeville and then make my way back home.

My apprehension had little to do with any perceived danger or struggle in the offing. It's not as though I was going to live in a remote wilderness. I was, after all, driving a car to a place that—if it was still standing—I knew had plumbing and electricity and a telephone. I had with me, as well, the radio/cassette player and would later find in an old wooden chest up in Wickerby's loft, a small black-and-white television set that, despite all my antenna manipulations and enhancements, got only one channel, which featured, of all things, nature shows.

Some might consider such devices gross impurities in the context of a place like Wickerby, but then I hadn't left Brooklyn to achieve some Thoreauvian ideal, to shed all inventions and conventions by way of arriving at a more essential self. Such endeavors—a modern man playing at primitivism—tend to be far more encumbered by self-consciousness and pretense than any truly plain existence is by its inherent hardships.

Some years ago, I traveled to the jungles of northern Peru to write a travel story for a magazine about life near the source of the Amazon River—yet another mission on behalf of the developed world to capture a lost essence, a vanishing way of being. For weeks I passed with my guide in a small dugout canoe down ever more remote Amazon tributaries. One evening, we arrived at a lone thatched hut built high on stilts above a half-moon bank of mud at the water's edge, thousands of miles of jungle pressing in at its back.

The Indian family living there—an elderly couple, their two sons, their wives and three small children, members of the local Shimaco and Cocamilla tribes—responded as though they'd been expecting us all along, inviting us up the ladder into their hut, the sons going off to catch fish for dinner, the women starting a fire.

The hut was just a single, open floor with an A-frame roof of tightly woven palmetto leaves and one wall setting off the back sleeping quarters. It was all built without nails. Everything was lashed together with a jungle vine called tambishi, but what I remember best about the place are its anomalies: the dated calendar of winter scenes on the bedroom wall, with X's drawn through the first few months of days until someone just stopped bothering; or the plastic cups, hanging from hooks on one of the hut's main stilts, rare, bright flowers against the jungle's unrelenting green; or the family's clothing, everyone dressed in the mismatched double knits, plaids and T-shirts with U.S. pro sport team logos on them that have by now made their way like so many migrating butterflies to the backs of the world's most remote people.

Everyone's outfit seemed to be their only one, washed and rewashed in the river and, where the fabric had given way, patched and sewn with what struck me as an unlikely precision and elaborateness until I was led into the back sleeping quarters. There, behind a hanging lace curtain, was the family's prized possession: an old Singer sewing machine, its wrought iron seat and filigreed treadle facing the open jungle like a sacred altar.

For me, Wickerby, too, stood at just enough of a remove from civilization to isolate inventions in this way, render them otherworldly, numinous: the radio I'd bring out each evening on a long extension cord and set upon the wooden table beside the stone cooking pit, letting the nightly news spill across an uncaring hillside; or the TV at night in the cabin, flickering against all that hilltop darkness like a lone, frenetic firefly; or my car, which, set off as it was to one side in the tall field grass, seemed no more than an aching arrangement of sun-struck metal.

My apprehensions about going to Wickerby had more to do, I think, with a basic fear of being alone in the dark, and the growing suspicion, soon to be confirmed, that no matter how far or fast I had traveled that first day, I had still not outrun the curse of that hole in my street.

It had been a fitful drive north. I-91 out of New Haven

through Connecticut, Massachusetts and Vermont is pretty much a straight shot, but then Lucy is not a good car dog. She'll start to settle as I slip into the higher gears, but should the road curve even slightly, she'll jump up and begin emitting a sound that the Pentagon might really consider putting to use. It's a high-pitched blend of a whine and a wheeze and instantly frays all the body's nerve endings. Between my fear of provoking that noise and the sight of Rasteedy all atwitter in the dashboard ashtray, I found myself driving like a pianist playing to a haywire metronome.

It was Rasteedy, I realize now, who bore the brunt of the upheaval in this neighborhood last spring; Rasteedy who was made to assume the role of miner's canary and alert me—via an alarming molting and egg-laying spree—to the serious decline in living conditions here. Lucy suffered as well, I'm sure. Pets, they say, register long before we humans do any serious disruptions in the status quo. It's just that in Lucy's case, aberrant behavior is often difficult to discern.

Lucy is a Dalmatian, a breed whose inherent skittishness has been greatly exacerbated in recent years by both the re-release of the classic Walt Disney animated feature *101 Dalmatians* and, most recently, the opening of a live-action version. This has not only resulted in intense over-breeding to meet sudden consumer demand for Dalmatian puppies but has also made it impossible for Lucy to go anywhere on the planet without being charged by hordes of children screaming "Pongo! Pongo!" with their parents pushing them forward to touch the living cartoon.

My own dignity—or is it vanity?—compels me to mention here that I was not party to this Dalmatian craze, although I will admit that I've often been tempted to capitalize on it. There have been times of dire financial need when only Lucy's disobedience has kept me from trying to get her some work in TV commercials and magazine ads, and times when that same disobedience has actually had me thinking twice about some of the incredible offers that have been tendered me for my dog. A guy in a tinted-glass, bauble-filled BMW pulled up alongside me at a stoplight on Washington Avenue one afternoon. He rolled down his window.

"Yo. Das a Domination, right?"

I nodded.

"Female?"

I nodded.

"Give you fifteen hundred for her."

I had, of course, every intention of saying no, when an appalled Bex leaned across the front seat and rolled up my window. I drove off daydreaming about the substantial return I would have made on my original fifty-dollar charitable outlay for Lucy to the Fireman's Fund.

Like Rasteedy (given to me by friends who misconstrued the preponderance of bird imagery in my poetry as a desire to own the real thing), Lucy was a gift from an acquaintance, a guy I hadn't seen since I was eight or nine years old, growing up in Flatlands in the early 1960s. I stepped into a bar beneath the elevated subway tracks outside Yankee Stadium late one night seven summers ago, and there he was, Patrick Featherston, the same face just lifted to an adult height.

He had, he told me, become a fireman, had just gotten married to a firewoman—becoming one of only two fire-fighting couples in the whole of New York City—and, to complete what seemed to be a mission to model his exis-tence after a children's book, he owned a Dalmatian that had just given birth to nine puppies, the runt of which I was just drunk enough to agree to take, sight unseen. I picked Lucy up the following day from Patrick's firehouse, located, it turned out, an easy stroll from here on the far side of Prospect Park.

I have, since that fateful day, often had to ask myself what it is exactly about spots that so excites people. "Spots!" the security guard at our local bank shouts every morning on my way to J's. "Inty!" cries the spindly old woman who goes up and down Washington Avenue all day in the same yellow Easter dress and matching bonnet, "I knew a dog like yours back in the sixties named Inty. You know, black and white—integration!"

Or perhaps it's the whiteness that so captivates, that mythic, Melvillian whiteness that, having already been randomly splattered in this case, moves people to further remark upon it, making Lucy a kind of four-pawed palimpsest of everyone's projected dreams, desires and per-sonal histories. On a bank line last spring, a woman ran up, hugged Lucy around the neck, and started crying out about her troubled homeland of Dalmatia.

Bex and I no longer take Lucy with us when we do our food shopping on the other side of Grand Army Plaza in the genteel environs of a tree-shaded, brownstone-lined neighborhood known as Park Slope, a place where the goods are neither rancid nor unreasonably priced, and the residents tend to have more time on their hands for, among other things, the facile activism of animal rights. People have broken into our car there to deliver Lucy from perceived abuse. "I've walked your dog," went one of the notes taped to my windshield. "I've given her water. Next time I'll take her from you."

Outside Park Slope's main supermarket one winter afternoon, Lucy caused a small riot when she started barking for my return, something she does no matter where I leave her except, for some reason, outside of Mr. J's. She had me on a particularly short leash that afternoon because it had been snowing, and although we'd just been romping together through the drifts in Prospect Park, waiting outside a supermarket for five minutes was clearly not on whatever dim little agenda my piebald purebred had set for herself.

The instant I disappeared from view, she began emitting a series of her best pathetic, strangled yelps, which, coming as they do from "Pongo," tend to attract all of the unassigned sympathy within a two-mile radius. I ran through that store, buying things to prepare for my dinner that I wouldn't feed Lucy just to get back out to her, when an announcement interrupted the Muzak: "Will the owner of the spotted dog please report to the front desk?"

I was met there by a garish-looking middle-aged woman. I remember the blond wig mostly, teased high above her head. She kept shaking her finger at me in front of six full checkout lines, saying over and over in a shrill voice: "You should have that dog taken from you!"

WICKERBY

By the time I got outside, I had to part a ring of onlookers four deep to get at Lucy, or to begin to get at her, wrapped as she was by then in sweaters and blankets, looking quite pleased, if a bit bewildered, by all the attention. Of course, had it been a homeless person, no one would have bothered, no one would have wanted to get tangled in the web of want and woe that comes with a human being.

I could see the wig moving back and forth behind the circle of accusatory faces pressed in all around me. She was calling for the police. I knelt there in the snow, trying to free Lucy from the layers heaped upon her; trying to get down, at last, to the dog, the dog who, as I began to stride off with her in righteous indignation, either punctuated my exit or entirely mocked it—I'm still not certain—by depositing a huge shit there on the sidewalk.

It's difficult to say anymore which of Lucy's maladies and behavioral tics are the result of her breed's rampant Disneyfication and which can be ascribed to this neighborhood: the allergies, eczema, colitis and leaky bladder. As for her severe myopia, this may be traceable to a night back in her first year when she ate one of the lopped-off rooster heads left over from a Santeria ritual in Mt. Prospect. If you ask me, she's been a little cock-eyed ever since.

Still, Lucy did seem particularly jumpy to me last spring, ever on the verge of one of her nesting frenzies: eyes wide, ears tucked back as if to invite the very disturbances that would set her off. Over at J's one morning, about a week before I decided to set out for Wickerby, I left Lucy, as I usually do, tied to the metal security gate that J draws in front of his store each night after closing. Inside, J was telling me about the pigeons in the apartment across from me, explaining how the landlord has no intention of evicting them, how he has, in fact, been waiting for the building's last human tenants to leave so that, in his own far-off dream of gentrification, he could eventually convert the building to co-ops.

In the interim, the pigeons have (like everyone else here, you could say) made the best of an otherwise bleak situation, finding their way in through the building's cracked, top-floor windows. J says the landlord had no idea they were even in there until the day he finally answered his holdout tenant's complaints about the strange smells and noises coming from across the hall. He apparently got the apartment door open only a few inches on a dense roomful of cooing and wing flaps and then locked the place up and hasn't been back since.

As J was talking, I remember a truck backfiring, and then, moments later, a tremendous swell of shouts and car horns rising directly in front of the variety store's newly built display window. The two of us ran outside to find J's security gate stretched straight out into the middle of Washington Avenue, the morning rush-hour traffic building on either side of Lucy, drawn up on her hind legs, her front paws furiously nesting the morning air.

We were a sorry troika, indeed, by the time I'd exited I-91 just shy of the Canadian border to buy gas at a northern Vermont town called Wells River. It was near sundown, and I headed toward a lighted sign above the treetops, P & H TRUCK STOP. There was one island of gas pumps and a single-story clapboard house with a COUNTRY STORE sign above the front door, and a row of benches set out front under a roof overhang supported by three white posts.

I filled up, then pulled the car in front of the store and went inside to pay for the gas and buy the flashlight I'd forgotten to pack. When I got back outside, I saw a woman standing at my passenger-side window with two little girls who were pointing and saying, "Look, there's Pongo!" Lucy was in the front seat now, in the throes, it appeared, of one of her nesting frenzies. Then I saw that the bird box was no longer in the ashtray.

For the next few moments, it was as if I were standing off to one side along with that woman and her daughters, watching myself in disbelief as I threw open the car door, saw Lucy hop in the back and then turn toward me, her face—I won't soon forget it—a lean, wolfish wince with one bird leg jutting out.

I pried her jaws open. A matted yellow pulp rolled briefly across my palm, then dropped to the ground. Grabbing Lucy by the neck, I pulled her from the car and dangled, with one arm, all fifty-five or so pounds of her straight out before me while a rather hastily concocted, interspecies justice code raced through my mind: a dog for a bird, a pet for a pet. Then I just tossed her into the backseat, picked up Rasteedy, put her and the crushed bird travel box in the bag that I'd exited the store with, placed the bag in the glove compartment and drove away, no

doubt leaving that woman and her children with a decid-
edly altered rendition of life with Pongo.

I am, by now, able to view this event far less apocalyp-
tically than I did at the time. In fact, once Rasteedy was in
the ground at Wickerby, and I far enough into my stay
there that I'd become completely dependent upon Lucy's
animal instincts as my defense against all threats, real or
imagined, I would stop behaving like those who routinely
project their emotions onto her. I was able reasonably to
ask myself what exactly I expected of Lucy: That she make
the same distinction I do between Rasteedy and other
birds? That she somehow understand Rasteedy's special
status as the other pet in my life? After months of nestling
up, night after night, against Lucy's warmth in the cabin
loft, and then sliding off to sleep in the faith that her
heightened senses would alert my dulled, civilized ones to
the approach of strangers—I am now able to tell myself
that I have Lucy, in part, because I depend upon the very
same impulses and responses in her that killed Rasteedy.

In the car with her that night, however, I could think
only of the slaughter, and of the ongoing curse of that hole
in my street. Nature itself seemed out of alignment, my
mind aswirl with images of lopped-off rooster heads, shot-
gunned zoo bears, stolen elms; of upturned streets and rest-
less Egyptian mummies in the bullet-riddled night; of
populous cities where people and pets hold on to each
other within stacked cells and ride out the hours, listening
to the caged birds sing duets with the free ones perched all
around them.

I drove frenziedly, the rolling Vermont farmland on either

side giving way now to straight, dense rows of pine like an army marching northward to the Canadian tundra. Just shy of the border there was a sign: 45 DEGREES LATITUDE— HALFWAY POINT BETWEEN EQUATOR AND NORTH POLE. I'd been driving all day north toward what seemed to be the very top of the globe, only to learn that there was a whole other quarter of it whorling coldly up ahead, pressing in on the back of a crumbling cabin that I was about to make my home.

At the border, the customs guard questioned me about the folded birdcage, and I related the whole gruesome tale. He nodded gravely and, before waving me on, bent down and peered into the back for a good look at the villain.

I headed straight into the open dark, trying to remember which way I was supposed to turn, trying to decide whether Lucy's actions were more indicative of the world I'd fled or the one I was about to enter.

IT HAD BEEN SIX SUMMERS since Bex first brought me to Wickerby, but I was somehow able to recall the route she took: the sharp left a short way inside the border through the town of Rock Island, past an old brick tannery built astride the Tomifobia River. Then straight west along a dark, narrow, two-lane thoroughfare that I remembered because the road itself is the border, the cars in the driveways of the houses on the left bearing Vermont license plates, and the cars on the right, Quebec ones.

The road ends at a T-intersection between Beebee Plains, Vermont, and its reflection, Beebee, Quebec, through which I passed, driving straight north again now, crossing a set of railroad tracks at the far end of town, and then taking the left fork opposite the last house in Beebee, its front lawn decorated—just as it had been when Bex and I passed it—

with giant grizzly bears carved out of tree trunks: one in a top hat and tux, clawing at the air; another smiling broadly with a bright blue fish pressed to its belly; and still another off at the lawn's far edge, walking on all fours, head down, into the darkness.

For the next five miles or more there are only a few farmhouses, their lit front porches coming in and out of view with the dips in the road, like boats on deep wave swells. At the last farmhouse, the road drops sharply to the base of a narrow inlet connecting the waters of Lake Memphremagog with Fitch Bay. I saw the old covered bridge and remembered Bex telling me about the huge country inn that used to stand beside it, dark green with gable roofs and dormer windows and a wraparound screened porch overlooking the bay. The night the place went up in flames, Bex said they could see the glow all the way from Wickerby's hilltop, and the whole family drove down the mountain to watch.

The road they took lets out just past the covered bridge. The way is dirt from there and steep, winding up through deep woods, the runoff from past rains having rendered the road surface a washboard of deep ridges that rattled the car and nearly made me spin out on turns. At the top of the hill, I came to an intersection—if the crossing of two dirt roads in the middle of a cow pasture can properly be called an intersection—and this was where my memory failed me.

Wickerby was only a mile or two away at that point. Off to my right, just out of view, was a cow pond and an old barn with a dirt road ramp leading right up into its hay loft so that trucks can back their bales straight in. Across the road from there stood the weathered gray toolshed in which Albert was forever tinkering with his tractor. Soon, I would come to know those places as one does the images of a favorite painting. Just then, however, I was driving into a void.

I decided to go straight ahead, past the barn and toolshed, up another steep, winding dirt road that delivered me, it seemed, a whole world higher among the endless stars, and it was there that I first understood how alone I was about to be, that I felt that crackling portent, from which cities shield us, of our ongoing insignificance.

The night air had the steely, high-pitched odor of snow. Stars arced down to the stubbled fields all around me, with only a thin, saw-toothed edge of pine tree tips visible along the horizon's brim. I edged the car further into that darkness, and then, over the next rise, saw Albert's farmhouse, my headlights igniting a brief spray of cow eyes on the hill behind his rooftop.

It was exactly like a winter's night I'd spent many years ago, driving through a snowy pasture in the Berkshires toward a cottage I'd never seen before. A friend had offered me the place to rent for the winter and spring. He wrote the directions on a cocktail napkin one night in a lower Manhattan bar, and, exactly as I'd do this past spring, but with none of the prompting, and no dogs, or canaries, or near-wives, I just picked up and left. One minute I was steeped in lighted concrete, the next I was alone in the mountains, staring at the very pasture gate my friend had described in the directions.

I propped it open with a field stone and then got back behind the wheel. Up ahead, in the far reaches of my head-lights, there was what looked to be a faint, low-slung con-stellation in the night sky except that the stars were jiggling slightly, and appeared to be coming, slowly, toward me. I tried blinking them back into alignment, and then I just put my head down on the steering wheel and awaited impact. Nothing. I looked up to see a semicircle of massive cow heads heavily adrift at the front bumper. They just held there, staring in at me. I honked the horn. Nothing. Finally, I touched my foot to the accelerator and nudged forward until the heads began to part.

Weeks later the local farmer who owned the herd explained that they'd mistaken my car for the feed truck. But all through that Berkshire winter and spring, those cows were never far off. Some mornings, I'd wake to find them at the cottage's bedroom windows, noses pressed to the sills, those huge eyes, unblinking, through which whole days pass uninterrupted. Before long, with no one else around up there to contradict me, I became convinced that I was just a dream the cows were having.

I coasted downhill toward Albert's place and then turned left onto the Wickerby road, thinking all the while that I'll never be able to stand that now, to remain alone that long within the blankness of a cow's eyes, within the wide, edge-less air of an unappointed day. Back then I still inhabited that grace period of youth in which the mind has not yet been divorced from the body, has not yet been alerted by the body's internal riots to the matter of its own mortality.

I remember days up at that Berkshire cottage when I felt—perhaps because I'd lived in my body less long—nearer to my own bones, felt such a full, weighty recline within myself that it seemed I could outwait a tree. There were days when, walking through the surrounding hills, I felt—because I'd lived on the earth less time—nearer to it as well, and I remember one spring afternoon in particular, after months of snow cover, standing at the base of the cottage's newly thawed back pasture, the steep, upward slope of which claimed just enough of the horizon to suggest the earth's round, slow revolve, and I couldn't help but go facedown and ride it for a while.

The older we get, I told myself, as Wickerby's road began to narrow, the longer the journey becomes back to that deep repose we once felt in ourselves and upon the earth, and, of course, we never quite get there. Through all of my days at Wickerby this was the feeling that I would keep coming back around to, and that haunts me still tonight: the gathering weightlessness and speed of living, the sense of lost gradualness.

It's a feeling that people always mistake for a larger malady, the perennially voiced complaint that life "moves too fast these days." I read in the newspaper just today about a group of urban and suburban dwellers who have defected from the "hurried pace" of modern life to go live with the Amish. "We've moved to a whole new speed in how we live," one of the group's leaders explained.

"We started with the horse and buggy, and then to the automobile, and now we're moving at electronic speed. We're finding that people can't live at that speed."

But you never hear the young complaining about the speed of life, except, perhaps, to say that it goes too slowly. Theirs, in fact, is the sort of irritable impatience with time's sluggishness that inspires the invention of the very mechanisms that will later leave them complaining about the loss of gradualness; that will leave them looking backward, as each advancing generation does, in an attempt to retrieve lost essences: noiseless dawns, and dying nomads, and collapsing log cabins; that will have them building log cabins on top of city high-rises, or putting log-cabin siding over new suburban prefab homes; or making museums and shopping plazas out of abandoned wharfs and factories and railway yards, places wherein we restore and display as artifacts the very machines that in their time made time seem to move too fast. All so that we might still visit with what we believe to have been a heavier, hands-on day.

In fact, what technology really does is make our days seem to move too slowly, the nonstop flicker and flight of all our mechanisms stranding us within what, by contrast, becomes an ever more static present. We, in other words, devise the illusion of our own discomfort even as we continue to make life easier. We resist our mechanisms even as we go on inventing them.

Outside my window now, I watch the La Guardia–bound jets drifting down into their port of air, think of the passengers who'll soon debark, walk metal gangplanks over runways through a terminal to their next mode of transport, the next vessel of speed that will deliver each of them—each same, slow, plodding vessel of flesh—back home; back to their own uniquely furnished share of this timeless present, a room somewhere inside of this mired, mincing measure of a night and a set of windows to sit by and stare out of with an age-old, deep-seated longing.

A short way along the Wickerby road, I arrived at a gate, one I hadn't remembered from the first visit, a long sapling with a NO TRESPASSING sign dangling from the middle. It's called "Rake's Gate." I found a photograph of it in the Wickerby album, the "Official Rakes Gate Photo": Bex and unidentified girlfriends on a bright summer day, all of them leaning against the sapling in cutoff shorts and T-shirts, Bex's heavily bearded father, a former British Royal Air Force pilot, standing imperiously by in his straw sun hat, long-sleeved white linen shirt and matching pants, a pair of bird-watcher binoculars dangling from his neck, his right arm propped stiffly upon a walking stick.

I stepped out of the car, the cold night air separating me just enough from my clothing to remind me of it. I opened the gate, then came around to the trunk and dug out a sweater. The car exhaust sounded frail in all that quiet, like isolated coughing in a vast concert hall.

Near the crest of the entrance road, I could begin to make out another ridge of pine tree tops along the western horizon. The road leveled off. I turned right, into the open field, Wickerby arriving at once with my headlights against the night sky like a slide projection from my own past.

It looked far stouter than I'd remembered or expected, a formidable wreck. It looked, in its isolation, like the very first house, the only house in the world.

The surrounding field was still matted with the weight of the last snow, so I drove right up to the cabin's dilapidated, A-framed entranceway, trying to leave as little of that huge night as possible between myself and the front door. For a moment, I just sat there, not wanting to turn off the car engine, as though it might never start up again, as though cars needed other cars around them to remember how to go. Lucy had that whining noise of hers worked up to an unbearable pitch. Then I turned the key. The silence rushed in, and I knew the odd business of staying had begun.

·THE·

WAY
AROUND

ON THE OAK DRESSER across from where I'm now sitting, there are two tall, thin wood statues of a Turkana man and woman. They look like long, dark late-day shadows cast across a bare earth. Bex bought them years ago during her first trip to Africa. They have crudely carved, uneven stands that cause them to wobble and wander slightly with any vibration: people walking through the apartment, subway trains passing six floors down, jet planes rumbling overhead on their descent into La Guardia Airport.

Weeks will go by and then one day Bex or I will notice that the statues have moved. We can mark their progress by the framed pictures on the wall directly behind them, black-and-white woodcuts from the Flemish artist Frans Masereel's 1925 collection "The City"—pictures in which the buildings, windows and combusted steam all have equal weight—the Turkana caught now, as though in wonderment, before the image of an arriving, steam-swallowed train; of a canal tug billowing smoke around a crowded stone footbridge; of a machinist dwarfed by the roomful of turbines he's polishing.

They'll wander, pause and, over the course of countless Brooklyn nights, turn to face the image of a lone construction worker at rest atop the high row of stones he's just laid into the city's newest, tallest building yet, his trowel held at his side, his head bowed, penitent, even as he brings us another step closer to the inimitable stars.

On TV now, the man in search of noiseless dawns is setting up his recording equipment in a dried riverbed somewhere in Africa. I'm half expecting Bex to walk by in the background: she following the crew that's following the vanishing nomads through the frame of the crew that's following the man who's gone in search of the world's last soundless sunrises.

I keep thinking of her out there somewhere tonight on the earth with the Turkana, the windblown seeds of a civilization that never take hold, "lives pared down to the simplest movements," Bex writes in one of the letters I found here upon my return yesterday, "always setting up and breaking down their camps, lives so taken up with surviving the wilderness and the constant drought, that it's impossible to know them or what exists of their culture. The anthropologist who advises the film crew tells me that they do carry on an inner dialogue, thoughts about where to move next, about where to find water for themselves and their herds. Of course, on film this doesn't look like much: people sitting around under thorn trees, staring off.

"Sometimes the tribal elders will cut open a sheep and read the intestines for some sign of where to go next, or they'll flip a pair of sandals in the air and decide based on the way they land. But no one has been able to delve into their thoughts about life or about death and what they think happens afterward. They shrug and say they don't know. They place so little emphasis on the unknown. They have little time for leisure or abstractions. . . ."

Outside my window, the city's lights are taking hold, the breeze-brushed, gently pulsating grid. An unknowable, self-perpetuating matrix that pivots at once around our will to stay in one place, to stop wandering, and the freedom, which staying affords us, to imagine, to wander in place.

It all looks to me tonight as I used to imagine it through that mumbler's eyes: like one monumental abstraction and yet no less natural for that. Why is a cemented aggregate of homes arranged in a tall, tight cluster any further from nature than Wickerby is, than one wooden home within the woods? Is it because the city is so thoroughly man-made? But we wouldn't call the towering carpenter ants' nest that I found one day in Wickerby's collapsing southeast corner "ant-made."

A skyscraper may not be the same as a tree, but one is no more natural than the other, and both are, in the end, habitable outgrowths of the same skyward longing. Birds make good use of either. So do we. We are no less natural than the next creature, except that thinking makes it seem so, makes us invent a place called nature from which we can think of ourselves as having been exiled, and into which we can constantly seek readmittance if only through the door of a collapsing cabin, or a film of vanishing nomads, or the airy portal of a noiseless dawn.

There is no such thing as nature. Wickerby would remind me of this. There is just the earth and us, the namers, standing upon it, naming those places without us, nature. The stars would have passed forever silently through the puddles of melted snow cupped there around me in Wickerby's field that first night had I not arrived to interrupt them, to look back up and call them a name.

Lucy bolted the instant I opened the car door, just disappeared into the darkness. It was as though she'd just remembered something, as though she'd suddenly realized her life with me had been little more than a detainment. I stood alone at the cabin door, nervously fumbling with the lock. It never even occurred to me to enter through one of the cabin's broken windows. Somehow, after all the hours of imagining Wickerby, I was approaching the actual place in the most addled, unimaginative way.

The lock tumblers, on the third or fourth try, finally clicked. When I undid the latch, the cabin's uneven pitch actually thrust the door open to me. I stepped inside. The smell was of musty wood laced with cold air—something between an old steamer trunk and a starry night.

A tiny red bulb twittered to my immediate left. I shined the flashlight. It was one of those sonic pest-control devices you see advertised in the back of magazines. Bex must have turned it on just before we left years ago. It looked rather ridiculous there on top of Wickerby's refrigerator, covered in mouse droppings. Still, it did answer my question about the electricity. Someone in Bex's family had been paying all these years to keep the juice running to a ruin. Now I had only to find the fuse box.

The fun-house tilt of the cabin's floorboards sent me right into the wooden kitchen counter beside the fridge, so I decided to hold there and run my flashlight beam around the place. I first checked the integrity of the floor above me, looking for any breaches in the eight hand-hewn cross-beams of spruce that support the upstairs sleeping loft.

To my right, just inside the front door, old winter coats and rain parkas hung from a set of accordion hooks. A sun-bleached wooden table, its ends folded down, was wedged beneath the boarded front window. Axes and shovels stood in a corner basket along with the scythe that Bex had me go at the uncut fields with six summers back, at the expense of my hands.

Midway along the north-wall bookshelves, the books had been set into a spill. They'd fallen over the love seat by the window with the plum tree branches outside. More were strewn across the floor, where they mingled with the contents of the toppled mahogany secretary: all the playing cards, the game boards and pieces of many an idle Wickerby night. The chairs around the corner oak table had been turned over as well. A paper kite had fallen from the rafters onto the tabletop. An old radio lay on its side beneath the loft steps.

It all seemed to have just happened, as though my entrance had interrupted a wild party, or rather, a party of the wild—some Alice-in-Wonderland-like tea party for Wickerby's many stowaways, the eventual inheritors of all our ruins, the parasitic lot of them carrying on within the weak pulsations of an ancient pest-control device.

For a moment, Wickerby, in all of its disuse and decay, seemed to me some eerie harbinger of a far-off future. It was like an abandoned ark, no one left at the helm. A foundered vessel overrun not by those creatures that we might have chosen to bring along with us, the big, land-based animals like Rudy the rhinoceros, and all the others lined up along the floor of Colonel Milligan's library, the ones with whom we've long competed for space on the planet and have by now all but displaced and dispatched to zoos and theme parks, but by the small, largely unseen creatures which our tenure on earth, for all of its apparent dominance, can neither control nor contain, the creatures that ride us and all the things that we build.

Not just the pigeons, starlings or sparrows to whom Brooklyn and Wickerby are merely differently shaped perches. Not just the porcupines and groundhogs, the rats, squirrels, mice, spiders, ants, worms and termites every-where wielding our splinters and crumbs, but the original splinters of life itself, the bacteria and the viruses. The life-forms that somehow got left out of all the other arrangements of living matter on this planet—whether it's a person, a python or a paramecium—and that naturally get left out of all of our romanticized renditions of that place we call nature, but that everywhere lie in wait to co-opt our lives by way of continuing their own.

In a sense, I saw there in that cold cabin's flash-lit mishmash of books and mold, Scrabble squares and dust, farm tools and termite chew, some version of the end of nature—not the version that we in our hubris now believe ourselves to be bringing about (as though one sick leaf could somehow dictate the fate of an entire tree), but the end of us. I saw, as I would ever more clearly throughout my days at Wickerby, how that ongoing, protean and often invisible force to which we've long affixed the name nature, will shed all names and us and spin on.

The fuse box was half hidden in the cabin's southwest corner, obscured by the rusted piping of the kitchen's smaller, potbellied woodstove, and an endless yard sale's worth of junk: old fishing poles, tennis and badminton racquets, random golf clubs, a badly frayed butterfly net and—most absurdly given the surroundings—an electric weed trimmer.

I flipped all the switches, heard the water pump and the chemical toilet kick in, the fridge warble, and the frozen timer on the stove buzz. It was like igniting long-dead embers. There was a light hanging from one of the cobwebbed rafters above me, just a bare bulb strung inside of a bottomless amber cider jug. I reached up, clicked it on.

Right away, I could begin to discern a workable home beneath the havoc. Somehow, just the cider jug's orange glow was enough to lend the windows—their tan batik curtains, faded by time and sunlight into near transparency—a straighter, sturdier look. The windows did the same, in turn, to the cabin's otherwise-skewed logs. It was as if Wickerby was now rallying all of its strength around frailties: the sudden light and its multiple reflections against the broken panes. Around my own uncertain will to stay.

In a long, rectangular wooden box set alongside the kitchen counter, I found some kindling piled atop a stack of logs. I was wary about starting up a fire before checking the stove's piping for blockages. Bex had told me all about the danger of chimney fires, especially in a dried-up old tinderbox like Wickerby. Still, the inside thermometer on one of the cabin's vertical support beams read 45 degrees, so I decided I'd set some newspaper and twigs alight and then go outside to see if the smoke was making its way through the chimney pipe.

I opened the door to the woodstove. There was a great white tuft of what appeared to be cotton seat stuffing piled high inside the stove bed, a dead starling resting atop it. It looked like something from a Joseph Cornell box: a bird fast asleep in a drifting cloud.

I lifted the starling free with a shovel, wrapped it in newspaper and brought it outside to the car, where Rasteedy still lay inside the glove compartment. Backing the car away from the cabin, I parked it on the far side of the Wickerby entrance road and shined the headlights on the base of the butternut tree that stands there at the top of the hill. I buried Rasteedy and the starling together beneath the butternut. Rasteedy's cage I hung on a branch above the grave. Throughout the spring and summer, with the cage door wired open, and the water and feed trays filled, all kinds of birds—flycatchers, goldfinches and blue jays, cardinals, black-capped chickadees and slate-colored juncos—would stop by.

Lucy returned from her wilderness debut that night with a face full of porcupine quills. She made no fuss about it. Didn't make a sound. Just crept into the cabin and lay down at the end of the hanging couch opposite the wood-stove. My smoke test seemed to indicate that there were no major obstructions in the stove piping, and by the time Lucy had crept home, I had a big fire going for her to settle down beside. I think she was a bit embarrassed.

Bex had told me about the same thing happening to her old dog Wally Wuzzum, how the porcupine's quills actually hook beneath the skin and have to be snipped at the back end in order to let the air escape before you can pull them free. I ran back out to the car, remembering that I'd put Lucy's nail clippers in the glove compartment. It was on my way back into the cabin, just beside the front door, that I first saw the woodchuck.

It was no more than fifteen feet away, half hidden within a small chink in the cabin's foundation, its head fixed straight ahead but its eyes regarding me, peripherally. It just held there, staring off, making no attempt to hide or flee, not even as I stepped closer, stepped into that warm, tensile repellency that builds on the air between you and a wild animal the closer you come to it. I couldn't help thinking that it had been there the whole time, watching my every step—the disgruntled host of that party I'd interrupted, trying now to assess my intentions.

Of course, isolation breeds such delusions, encourages the indulgence of every fantasy. This is especially so at a place like Wickerby, which, even now, remains more myth to me than matter, a place far longer spoken and thought about than lived in. Sitting at the window with the plum tree branches one day, I actually began to compose a libretto between a wasp and a fly trapped against the upper pane. At night sometimes, listening in bed to the bats in the loft, I'd convince myself that I was becoming fluent in bat-squeak.

But standing there outside the cabin that first night, inching ever closer to this preternaturally stolid, unflinching woodchuck—near enough, at one point, to feel again that childhood urge, that deep tug of our ancient hunter-gatherer genes, to pick up a stone and kill the animal—I was suddenly filled with the same unsettling feeling I'd gotten upon first entering the cabin, a presentiment of some far-off future within that present-day ruin. I sensed thousands of tiny eye pairs peering at me from the cabin's walls and floorboards and loft eaves, and from the darkness of the surrounding woods. It was as though they were staring back at me from a world that we humans helped to shape, that we informed, but long ago fell away from: a world—and then a phrase I'd not thought of for years suddenly came back to me—of fearless forests.

WICKERBY

I went inside to free Lucy from her beard of pneumatic barbs. As soon as I finished, she started to investigate her new home, going from smell to smell, anointing Wickerby with her newly liberated nose. As for myself, there was so much for me to do that night by way of getting settled that I decided to do none of it. I slipped into a thermal union suit, threw a few more logs into the stove and then collapsed on the couch with a big bourbon—that reliable shortcut back to lost repose.

The quiet was enormous. I could almost hear the stars seething in their distant sockets. The cabin seemed to be trying to resituate itself around me—around my still-racing blood and the steady thrum in my ears. Everywhere, in scuffling increments, the mice were reclaiming their hold. Along with the woodstove's mounting heat came the un-forgettable essence of baked snake slough and cobweb. On the underside of the floorboards beneath my feet, I felt a slow, vibratory rubbing, as though of a heavy wire brush wielded by a drunk. A porcupine, I later determined, din-ing on the cabin's insulation.

I poured myself another bourbon. That woodchuck, I felt certain, was still keeping his vigil, watching me from somewhere along the foundation's rim. I sat there thinking about a world of fearless forests, remembering the time I followed a man who was following the world's last wild jaguars through the jungles of Central America, trying to learn enough about their habits and range to have land put aside for them, a last place upon the planet away from us.

On two thin poles now in a sudden clearing in the Cockscomb Basin of southern Belize, there stands a small wooden sign, the words burnished across it designating the surroundings: THE COCKSCOMB FOREST RESERVE—JAGUAR PRESERVE. I remember the first time I stood before it, thinking how absurd it looked and, in turn, made all of us look: the declaration of a halt to ourselves, a small promise to a vast, moiling jungle, of our willful cessation.

In his three years at Cockscomb, "El Hombre Tigre," as the Belizeans often referred to him, caught eight jaguars. He named each after a god from ancient Mayan mythology, in which the jaguar was held as a sacred animal, inhabiting a shadowy realm between earth and sky, between man and the gods. He put radio collars around the jaguars' necks and tracked them with a transmitter through the jungle, sometimes using a biplane to follow them from above.

But in the time it took him to get the reserve established, he would see all of the jaguars he followed disappear. Most succumbed to disease, parasites or infection. One was shot by a rancher, another by a local villager. Two others wandered outside the range of his radio receiver. He also lost one of his assistants to the bite of a deadly pit viper known as a fer-de-lance, nearly died himself once when his tracking plane caught the top of a tree upon takeoff and nose-dived into the jungle, and he had his life threatened numerous times by local villagers, descendants of the ancient Maya, many of whom didn't understand why they had to be relocated to make room for an animal they shoot when they come across it in the wild.

"To them," he would often tell me, "what I do with jaguars is unnatural. They think I'm a rich white man playing with wild animals, playing out a fantasy. It's hard for people here to understand." Not far from the reserve, in fact, he helped erect a zoo in the middle of the jungle so that local people could go and see their own wilderness, could begin to regard at a safe, abstract remove the very animals they live beside.

At night, in El Hombre Tigre's jungle hut—smaller even than Wickerby, just a room with a screened porch and a kerosene lantern weakly fluttering against the darkness— we'd talk about this, our mistimed planet, the staggered pacing of different cultures and their conceptions of the world that leaves a so-called modern man flying alone above a jungle, through that once mythic realm between earth and sky, trying to re-instill in the present-day descendants of the Maya their own ancestors' reverence for what has become to many of us a sacred animal again, a symbol of that equally mythic, other world we call nature.

I remember him telling me during our last night there, the two of us sitting up in the lantern light, trying, in the awful heat, to find sleep at the bottom of a bottle of Scotch, that he knew jaguars didn't have much longer, nor did any of the larger, land-based animals requiring significant acreage for survival. Still, he had managed to set up the reserve, and soon, he would be off to the Golden Triangle of Southeast Asia to follow an endangered species of tiger there, and then on to Taiwan to follow for a while in the fast-vanishing footsteps of the clouded leopard.

He told me he was spending his life this way for what we both agreed was, in the end, a purpose so fine as to be too easily dismissed by much of the world: trying to preserve on the planet a certain essence, what he described that night as "a sweetness" at the heart of a primeval fear, that he first felt in Belize the day he was walking a wide path through the jungle and, cresting a hill, came upon his first jaguar. He said he knew from the way it was just waiting for him, fully aware of his approach, that it had never seen a human being before. It held there, staring at him for a while, then padded off into the jungle.

We didn't see a jaguar in my weeks of hiking through the Cockscomb. We were, however, once very close on the trail of one: fresh tracks, an edgeless, exhilarating fear that grew with the sound of faintly breaking brush just ahead, and then, suddenly, behind us, the jaguar, as I was told they often do, having doubled back to trail us for a while, the whole proposition turned inside out, we now the anonymous, the observed ones, alone on the animal's terms.

All that night, El Hombre Tigre talked about the feeling of being alone with something that is so much more powerful than you and yet not threatening you; about the incredible difference between walking into a forest informed by the presence of a top predator causing fear in every creature below it, and one that's not. That's when I first saw it clearly—the world we're rapidly shaping now, the world of fearless forests.

Upstairs, I chose the brass bed that Bex and I had slept in years back, made up exactly as we'd left it, the same comforter resting atop the same bottom sheet, icy and stale.

It was like going to bed in an old wedding pastry. I turned on the caged plumber's light hanging from the bedpost above me so I could keep an eye on my axe atop the old steamer trunk. Lucy was so cold she'd practically pawed her way inside my union suit.

It took me forever to fall asleep. I couldn't get that thrumming out of my ears, the awful sound of the quiet, I told myself, and then Bex's voice came to me: "That's the city you're hearing," she whispered as we sat up in the loft that first summer night six years ago, unable to sleep. "It takes weeks for it to fall away."

I stared up at the swirls and knots in the cedar roof beams overhead, imagining how Bex must have done the same as a child, followed the same striations of wood into sleep. She knows I'm here, I kept thinking. She's asleep now somewhere near dawn on the African plains, having felt the pass of my flashlight beam inside the cabin, me a prowler now, a mere stowaway in this vessel of her past.

I lay there thinking of my nights back here in the city, nights when I'll often be awakened by an ongoing silence. For a moment, it's as though the whole city is in doubt, as if it will all have to be reinvented again by morning, and then something—just a faint siren wobbling like a tired top down a distant side street—saves it all from extinction and leaves me sitting up for hours, listening to the ensuing, random celebration of objects.

Nothing here to save now, I thought, staring up at Wickerby's roof beams, nothing to save. I heard a distant, passing car way down by Albert's, unraveling air from the trees, then nothing. I lay there falling through the quiet, falling, trying to follow the striations of cedar into sleep, thinking about Bex in Africa, thinking about the Turkana statues back here on the oak dresser top, wondering how many nights of city noise it would take to drive them over the edge, and how many nights of silence, me.

IN BEX'S RECURRING Wickerby nightmare, she comes up the entrance road and finds people everywhere, walking around the land and inside the cabin. They take things: the brass beds, the oak table and chairs, the games and books, the journals and photo album. They take photos and videos of Wickerby, as though already memorializing the place.

Bex screams at them to leave, but they don't notice her, being but phantoms of property—of any attempt to possess a part of this planet; stake a claim to it with a name and with enough time invested there, whether it's one spring and summer or an entire lifetime of prolonged stares and daily walks, and posted signs, and dug side gardens of perennials, blooming, and now, beneath the butternut tree, one pair of buried, moldering birds.

"I'm happier where I am," Bex would lie to me now if

I could somehow tell her tonight about the imminent collapse of Wickerby, if I could dial up that Rift Valley phone booth and leave the rings dangling for her to hear somewhere out there near the dawn of humanity. "I'm happier wandering," she'd say in that peevish, preemptive tone she always adopts when she's hurt, "happier not to have to hold to any one place long enough to see it lost."

"We moved camp this morning," she writes in one of her letters, "and there was a lot of debate over what to do with my goat. I have a goat because I saved a girl's life; at least her uncle believes I did. About eight days ago a young pregnant girl came to our camp complaining of terrible cramps. She hadn't eaten in five days. I went over to her and saw that her uterus was contracting severely and suggested we try to get her to a hospital. One of the film crew workers agreed to take her and off they went, only to return later that night. The clinic said that it was just a really bad case of morning sickness.

"The following morning, the director of the movie came to my tent and said the girl had lost the baby during the night and could I go see her. We drove over to her camp, knocking over trees to get there. I found her leaning against a friend. Beside them was a six-month-old fetus, dead, with some of the afterbirth but not all. I took her pulse—shallow. I looked into her eyes—pinpricks. She was ice cold and had no sense of where she was. I removed the rest of the afterbirth, wrapped up the girl and her dead baby and carried her—none of the men helped—to the truck. The girl was clinging to me. Again we took her to the clinic. This time they said they were not equipped, so we drove her on to a hospital in Lodwar. I'm amazed she lived.

"After we left her I thought certain I would cry but strangely they would have been crocodile tears. Handling the fetus, feeling around for her afterbirth didn't seem as frightful to me as it might have been if I were in a living place or a place where a good deal more is expected of life. Here so much is already dead that death is part of the landscape and hardly gruesome. When a Turkana dies they just prop the body in the crook of a tree and let the hyenas eat it."

When I finally fell asleep that first night at Wickerby, I dreamed that a city rose up around Rasteedy and the starling's grave, a city rising from the seeds of a caged bird and a free one, from the simple need to memorialize a possession's passing.

"The city of the dead antedates the city of the living." I wrote that down one day in my notebook, a sentence that someone had underlined years ago in Lewis Mumford's *The City in History*, a copy of which I found one day on Wickerby's shelves, one of the many books I'd riffle through up there with that heightened thief's attention one pays to another person's book collection. Entire pages had been highlighted from that particular section about how the world's earliest wandering tribes first settled around the monuments and mounds they erected for their dead: the city beginning therefore as a mere echo of our desire to visit the next world, one we can only imagine, or symbolize here with inscriptive stone.

Far out my window now, I can see the lights of lower Manhattan, the table of towering crystal clustered where once only a few huts like Wickerby stood, and wood fires against the darkness, and some gravestones.

This city, I would tell Bex tonight, is the best home I could offer her, one that isn't mine or anyone else's to give, as near to eternity as we'll ever come, an illusion of permanence in which each of us briefly shares.

WHEN I OPENED MY EYES in the loft bed on that first Wickerby morning, my body was sand, a stretch of wet, wave-pounded sand. Lift one hand, I kept telling myself, and then knead the rest of yourself into existence, but there would always be the next soft concavity of sleep to collapse into and explore. Not home, I kept thinking with each slow-fading wink toward wakefulness, not Brooklyn, but some wide wooden stadium of birds. I'd never heard such a depth of perfect thoughtlessness, deafening even through the closed upstairs dormers: an auditory pointillism on a wide-open canvas.

I lay there for hours, my body collecting on all the sleep debts accrued over countless city nights, millions of tiny alarm-laced skylines dissolving in my blood. I outslept

Lucy. She'd get up, stretch, paw about my lifeless bulk and then collapse down next to it again. I outslept slugs.

It was past noon by the time I stumbled downstairs and checked the small wind-up clock that I'd left the night before atop a tin of woodstove matches. I felt a bit embarrassed about getting up so late, but then I couldn't quite decide what exactly I was late for. Breakfast, surely, but who was checking, and just plain late, I suppose, to be entering a day, but then Wickerby's was a day whose doors were all ajar to begin with, rendering every entrance equally worthy and insignificant.

Before going to bed that first night, I'd hooked the cabin's front-door chain to a nail hammered into the right doorpost just beneath the telephone. I would do this every night throughout my stay as yet another precautionary measure against the crazed axe murderer, but it soon became a measure of an entirely different kind. Each morning I'd find the chain drawn a bit more tautly than I'd left it. This, it eventually dawned on me, was due to cabin shift—Wickerby's slow, inexorable list into oblivion. I worked out the rate of collapse to be roughly one chain link a week. With sixteen links of slack to play with at the outset, I figured I had just enough to keep me safe all summer from the axe murderer, provided, of course, that the cabin didn't kill me first.

Lucy, when I undid the chain, tore into the day and, just as she had the night before, completely missed the woodchuck, back at its post, vigilant and unwavering. I was getting a bit impatient with this woodchuck, if only for not behaving as any self-respecting woodchuck in that situation would, and thus putting me in the awkward position of having to interpret its motives.

At the window with the plum tree branches one day, I came upon a passage in Thoreau's *Walden* in which he describes walking home through the woods near dark with a string of fish when he catches a glimpse of a woodchuck stealing across his path. He felt "a strange thrill of savage delight, . . . was strongly tempted to seize and devour him raw."

That particular urge, I confess, never struck me with my woodchuck, but I did, as I've said, experience a similar primordial stirring during our previous night's encounter, a brief reversion to what Thoreau later describes as "the hunter stage of development," through which "even in civilized communities, the embryo man passes," and in which, I might add (and I think Thoreau, had he been able to visit my neck of Brooklyn last spring, would have agreed), even the fully evolved man sometimes gets stuck.

But whereas his Walden woodchuck, by fleeing, held up its end of the human/wild animal compact, my Wickerby woodchuck stood its ground, leaving me to read entirely too much into its presence, to consider in that untenable silence all other stages of human development.

I scrolled back through time, past low-lit, Museum-of-Natural-History, Dawn-of-Man dioramas. I saw Lucy (not my dog, of course, but Australopethcine, the oldest known hominid, the first upright Savannah walker, whose bones were found on the shores of the very Lake Turkana about which Bex has been treading all these months). Lucy and her hominid companion, striding in the general direction

of this fitful course we humans have been bound upon—
from nomadic hunter-gatherer, to settled farmer-villager, to
city-dweller, to what we have now, by and large, become:
urban naturalists, temporary keepers of the fearless forest,
the very forest into which (in my newly minted isolation
delirium) I suddenly fancied that woodchuck to be my
assigned escort, crouched there beside the cabin door,
patiently awaiting my appearance in order to rear up on
its squat haunches and at last declaim, "Sir, I give you
Wickerby."

On either side of the cabin's front door, huge burdock
plants had worked their way through the entranceway's
broken windowpanes, the dried stalks crisscrossing above
my head like the staffs of a royal guard. I hadn't noticed
them in my haste to get into the cabin the night before and
actually had to duck down a bit as I stepped outside.

A high, early-afternoon sun baked the matted fields all
around me, heat waves briefly wobbling up everywhere
into the day's prevailing chill. I walked out toward the
stone fire pit built about a hundred yards from the cabin's
front door at the crest of Wickerby's hill, the wooden
benches and chairs there facing out across the wooded valley between Wickerby and the upward-sloping pastures of
Albert's farm.

The day seemed too wide, each of my steps only pointing up the course that I wasn't taking, like those first words
you put down on a blank page. I walked out a bit further,
toward the wire birch to the right of the fire pit. Then I

stopped and addressed for the first time, head on, that deep feeling of disappointment, not in, but from the day, the knowledge of having no business there, no appointment.

There was only the barest hint of spring, a spray of luminescent buds against the pervasive browns and grays of winter. To the left of the wooden benches and chairs, a broken canoe lay rotting beneath a giant lilac bush that rings the base of a century-old sugar maple. By the end of May, that tree would be dancing in a purple hula skirt. Just then, however, I could see right through to its trunk, a metal sugar tap still protruding from the rivulets of bark. The field behind the fire pit brimmed with tansy and gold-enrod the last time Bex and I had seen it. Now it was all brown stubble and broken stems, like the rusted armature of a once-grand edifice.

Albert had clearly been coming up in the warmer months to mow for hay because the land around Wickerby still retained suggestions of order within its general disar-ray. From the outer edge of the cabin's north-wall plum trees, Albert had mowed clear to the line of poplars and oaks that buffer Wickerby from the neighboring farmer's upper pastures. He'd mowed a broad swath behind the cabin along the thicket of birches and blackberry brambles concealing the shores of Lake Y-Not (Bex's father's name backward). And then he'd worked his way back toward the front along the cabin's south side, somehow maneuver-ing his bushwhacker's wide blade in and around all the obstacles there: the row of massive white pines, which, in another month, would have a wide spray of white aster blooming at their shadowy base, and the rotting A-frame toolshed, and the big butternut tree at the top of the entrance road where I'd buried Rasteedy and the wood-stove starling.

I stood for a long time that first day out by the fire pit, just looking back at Wickerby—the weathered gray slant and shrug of it against the open sky and the surrounding fields declining into outlying bramble and woods. It looked absurd against my mind's fixed image of this city, and yet oddly noble. I felt I wasn't worn and tired enough yet to inhabit the place, to deserve its simple grace, its one essential reward. I felt I should put in a hard day's work and then return to it.

Just to the right of the doorway, directly above the head of that ridiculous woodchuck, I could see the word WICKERBY burnished into a block of wood dangling from a rusted metal sign post.

Poking around the bookshelves one day, I found some loose photos of the cabin before it was "Wickerby," when it was still the hub of a working farm. Alone and spare atop the hill, the place looked like a Revolutionary War fortress with little foot-square gun-holes for windows to prevent the escape of precious heat.

It was Bex's father who cut into the cabin's logs to build the big, shuttered ground-floor windows and upstairs dormers around which Wickerby now creaks. It was Bex's uncle who planted the north-wall plum trees and the pines in back, the mountain ash that shades the front right of the cabin, and the roof-high row of lilac and for-sythia that now swallows the front left—all the tree roots holding in the ground water that has undermined the cabin's foundation. A price was paid for trying to romanticize a utilitarian past. And there I stood, poised to be the next in a long line of idle occupants, hoping that Wickerby would hang on long enough to indulge one more.

If it fell right now, I wondered, and all the creatures that have become one with the cabin's walls were to come scurrying out, the mice, ants and termites, the spiders and the snakes—including the by-now-distant cousins of that baby brown snake that plopped from the loft rafters into Bex's lap one night six summers ago just as we were sitting down to dinner; if the cabin fell over and all that was left was infrastructure and underpinnings—a wind-mussed head of exposed wires and pipes and tilted posts—would I be able to go on like the man downstairs in his house of refuse? Would I be able to draw from Wickerby's open, uninhabited spaces the same strength that he seems to from these dreaming spires and hurried crowds?

I walked around the cabin's north side and across the back field, where I came upon a narrow path that winds down through the blackberry brambles and birches to the shores of Lake Y-Not. Lucy went bounding ahead of me and startled two geese from the water's edge: thick, ropy wing flaps and clamant tongues rising above the far-shore trees. A moment later, the silence closed around me, and then I heard faint rings rising like offertory bells into the vaults of a great cathedral.

I ran back toward the cabin, thinking that it must be Bex phoning from Africa or perhaps Brooklyn. Lucy ran alongside me, and upon reaching the cabin door, she of course seized that opportunity to notice the woodchuck and pounce upon it. Finally, one animal doing what it was supposed to. The woodchuck quickly followed suit by retreating, just in time, beneath the foundation. I picked up the receiver. A man's voice asked for Albert. I remembered then Bex telling me that Wickerby's phone is on a party line. Albert's place, as I would decipher over the coming weeks, gets one short ring, the farmer up the road two short, and Wickerby one long. I apologized and hung up.

It didn't take me long to put the cabin to rights, or, at least, to arrive at a workable detente with the dirt and decay. The first order of business was to get the water running. I could hear the water pump working, but nothing was coming through the tap. Arming myself with a flashlight and one of the pairs of rubber boots I'd found inside the cabin— they were all carefully lined up beneath the loft steps, as though Bex and her family had just gone off to bed—I lifted the trapdoor in the floorboards beside the woodstove and passed, reluctantly, down into the dark province of the porcupines.

A white, hoary layer of rotting insulation hung all around me. Shining the flashlight, I could see that the ground fell off sharply to my right into a muddy pond. The sound of trickling water on the far side seemed to indicate a leak in the line running between the pump and the kitchen faucet. The problem would be getting to it. I had to be careful not to bump any of the wood cribbing, which, as far as I could tell, was all that was keeping Wickerby from crushing me on the spot, or any of the loping strands of electric wiring whose insulation had been gnawed off here and there by the porcupines. Porcupines, I would learn, feast on whatever we humans can fabricate, the more synthetic, it seems, the better. Fiberglass, plastic, rubber are all delicacies to them. It wasn't until my car overheated one afternoon on the way into the States to buy groceries that I realized they'd eaten through the engine's water hoses.

Thankfully, the cabin's thick plastic water pipes had been spared. I found a separated elbow joint in the line leading to the kitchen sink, reattached it and then secured the whole arrangement with some duct tape. Back at the sink, I turned on the tap. There was a series of violent jolts, and rust-colored regurgitations, and then came a clear, ice-cold, glistening stream of what Bex likes to call "the healing waters of Wickerby."

It is remarkable how readily one's spirit rallies around the simple sight of running water. I set to work first on the refrigerator. Whatever had been left inside had long since evolved into entirely new life-forms, and I had to spelunk my way through them. That done, I took care of the toppled books and furniture, the scattered cards and game pieces, set them all back into place. I then went around gathering up butternuts. Slightly smaller than a walnut, with dark, craggy outer shells, they all had the same telltale bore where a mouse had gnawed its way to the reward inside. I found butternuts everywhere, piled in the corners, in old trunks and dresser drawers, strewn along the loft rafters. They filled three huge garbage bags.

I next began with a badly withered broom what loomed as an endless sweeping job until I reached the corner by the fuse box and discovered beneath all the clutter there an old, drum-shaped industrial vacuum. A quick splice of its severed power cord, and I was soon taking back Wickerby, freeing the rafters of their gossamer skeins, making notable inroads in the mice droppings and the termite chew.

Still, it's a hopelessly ill-defined proposition, cleaning a ruin. There's no real way of knowing when you're done, and all those creaturely encroachments that a house is designed to keep at bay have advanced so far that the prospect of wiping them out with one swipe of a vacuum wand leaves you confronting the kind of existential questions that can ruin a good day's cleaning.

I'd certainly set out with conviction, spurred on by remembrances of my post-Brooklyn, suburban upbringing: gleaming Formica countertops; lone silverfish straying across the blanched, Cometed expanse of a bathtub; my father rushing about the house with a rolled-up newspaper after one fly—"Damn fly!" fly in the ointment—while outside the neighborhood's soft-curbed lawns awaited the restoration of silence. But this being a preposterous standard to apply at a place like Wickerby, I soon lost all resolve.

I grew listless, anarchistic, sucked dirt off deeper dirt, took some insects and their houses, left others, determining fates randomly, like a tornado, like an act of God. At times, the vacuum nozzle would knock out sections of mortar between the logs, springing whole new daylight leaks. When I turned the vacuum off, I swore I could hear the sound of insect advance.

WICKERBY

· · ·

Wickerby is the kind of place that forces you to rethink your definition of an acceptable comfort level, to reconfigure the minimum distances that you require between yourself and the creeping non-you in order to get through a day. People—those of the developed world, at least—will often speak about wanting to abandon modern comforts and amenities and get back to "Nature," but when such a pilgrimage results, as it invariably does, in too close a communion with the creaturely, the pendulum tends to swing back the other way.

Having experienced equally horrid extremes of this human-comfort equation—the jungle and the suburbs—I was able to establish at Wickerby an uncommonly comfortable living arrangement between myself and my fellow DNA assemblages, one predicated, I'd say, on the principles of mutual wariness and avoidance. Of course, until we all became familiar with one another's schedules, there were a number of collisions which required of me a drastic resetting of my natural recoil and shudder gauge.

This is not to say that I ceded all authority to my cohabitants—let them literally walk all over me. I've never been able to master the nearly bovine insouciance that, for example, I've seen inhabitants of the Amazon exhibit when subjected to the barrage of creatures that exist there.

I remember my first night in a small jungle village along the Tahuayo River called Esperanza: forty or so wood huts situated around a single-story cement schoolhouse; a village set on a gentle rise above the river and somewhere out of time, barely interrupting the wilderness. White and golden-brown longhorn cattle grazed in the open fields between Esperanza's huts. There was often a slight breeze throughout the day, the smell of firewood, and bread baking in domed clay ovens under palm-thatched roofs. At one end of town, a dirt path led through a dark column of trees to a small white chapel.

After we dined that night on one of the village chickens, the owner of the hut I was staying in converted his place into a bodega—a distinction he instantly achieved by pinning a gold-tinseled FELIZ NAVIDAD streamer over his door (Christmas decorations were all he had) and then starting up the gas-powered generator that he kept under a blanket in his sleeping quarters to power the colored bulbs strung on a limp wire along his front porch's palm eaves. The night would be over when we ran out of gas.

We were all gathered there on his porch, my guide and me and some of the village men, drinking beer and playing sapo—"frog"—a popular Peruvian game that involves trying to throw lead coins into the mouth of a little metal frog screwed into a table. All around the frog are holes through which coins can drop into a catch-drawer below, a coin through the smaller holes nearest to the frog worth as many as fifteen hundred points, and the larger ones on the table's periphery as little as one hundred. Getting a coin in the frog's mouth, which is almost impossible, is worth four thousand points, and the first to reach fifteen thousand is the winner. It may not sound like much, but on a slow, hot night in the

Amazon, you can spend hours trying to get that frog to swallow a coin.

Afterward, we sat up talking, the hut's owner telling a story about the time the U.S. Army sent soldiers into the jungles there after World War II to engage in war games with the Peruvian Army. In the first exchange, the Americans marched in and established their position. Two hours later the Peruvians entered, promptly staked out the Americans and surrounded them. In the second exchange, the Peruvians marched in, and the Americans followed. They walked right into a well-concealed ring of Peruvian soldiers simulating various jungle noises and got ambushed. The third interlude was staged at night. The Americans went in first this time and tried to immerse themselves in the brush as the Peruvians had, but they were overrun by bugs, snakes and bats and left before the Peruvians could arrive.

As the owner spoke, I looked around in the glow of what were perhaps the only lightbulbs for hundreds of miles, and saw a similar array of creatures surrounding us: crickets and moths, mosquitoes and dragonflies; countless lizards scurrying across the porch's wood railings; toads jumping through the grass, vampire bats madly circling the hut as though on some high-speed merry-go-round—the myriad noises of a jungle night assuming tangible shapes. At one point, a large, shiny, black beetle crash-landed into my lap. The owner picked it up as he continued talking and rolled it around like a marble on his pant leg. I think I was waiting for someone to say that this was just not an environment for humans to live in, but everyone sat there, an occasional lazy slap of the hand rearranging the hot bug swarms alighting all around us. With the low, weak sputtering of the generator, it was as if we were trapped in an overcrowded lifeboat, barely afloat above the teeming continuum.

I remember my guide looking somewhat amused by it all, he who lived in a nice house back in Iquitos, the house he'd bought with his earnings as an intermediary between the opposing quadrants of our mistimed planet; as a guide for those like myself who live in places civilized and comfortable enough to afford the idleness that breeds the desire to visit less civilized, less comfortable environs. He makes a good living giving us—the only animal that advances by looking backward—a few salutary peeks at the primitive.

I wandered drunkenly through Esperanza late that night in search of the hut I was to sleep in, the Tahuayo's black water glinting beneath a full moon, a few cooking fires still glowing against the jungle. I lay down at one point in the grass on a hill overlooking the river. I remember feeling at that moment such an unlikely affinity with the unfamiliarity of my surroundings that I secretly began to construct a version of my life there, hoping all the while that no one would hold me to it. Fall asleep here on this spot, I thought, and you'll wake up an Esperanzan; fall asleep here, I thought again, noticing now the long line of carrier ants passing at my feet with their outsize nest pieces, and you'll be soon be rendered ant-chew.

"The ants just carried his fingers away," I remember El Hombre Tigre telling me one morning as we cut our way with machetes through the jungles of the Cockscomb, the

WICKERBY

undergrowth there having grown unchecked since loggers hauled off the shade of the taller mahoganies. (This would result in an unlikely bit of symbiosis between man and wild animal, the Cockscomb's thick undergrowth providing an abundant food source for peccaries, pacas, tapirs and armadillos, all favorite prey of the jaguar.)

We had stopped at the edge of an old logging road where years earlier one of the local Indians who'd been hired to help track jaguars lost three fingers on his right hand when he got them caught between the chain and drive sprocket of an old motorbike he was trying to repair. He rushed back to the base camp to have the bleeding stanched and his hand wrapped, and then El Hombre Tigre had the tracker lead him back to the site of the accident in an attempt to recover the fingers for their emergency flight in the tracking biplane to the hospital in Belize City.

"Two fingers were already gone when we got there," he told me, "and the ants were carrying the third one away."

Lie down here, I remember thinking as we pushed further into the Cockscomb that morning, and it wouldn't be long before the forces competing for survival made use of you: the endless conveyor belts of carrier ants; the mosquitoes and the viruses—the dengue and malaria—that they carry; the sand flies and screwworm flies whose larvae eat live flesh; or the botflies that deposit their larvae upon mosquitoes, which transfer them in turn to us, the larval grub worms breeding beneath your skin until they eventually burst forth from pus-filled nooks, pincers grasping.

Jaguars, I was told, go to great lengths to establish and mark off their own territories in order to avoid skirmishes because in such a parasite-ridden environment like the Cockscomb, no fight between jaguars can have a winner. The slightest wound invites infestation and death. One morning, El Hombre Tigre noticed a small cut over the eye of a pig he'd secured in a trap. He'd intended to return that afternoon with disinfectant, but torrential rains washed out the roads. A day later, the pig's eye was gone, an empty socket filled with screwworm larvae.

Nothing lives long where everything lives so vehemently. Zoo jaguars have a much longer life expectancy than do wild ones, but they live, we feel safe in saying, not nearly so well. We, the inhabitants of the tamed, "overdeveloped" world, live longer than the people of the Cockscomb or the Amazon, but we live, some would say (of us city-dwellers, anyway), too much like zoo animals, pacing back and forth in our allotted cells.

And yet who, I asked myself, standing there in the cabin that first day, overwhelmed by the wreckage, poised to surrender to Wickerby's ever-advancing marauders, who would seriously claim that our rightful place is back among the jaguars in a paradise of parasites? I have heard the absurd declension by which those who think civilization has advanced too far try to sift back through previous stages of human progress, to peel away the layers of our inventions and advances in order to return to that point where they feel we last lived in harmony with nature—as though such a condition or place ever existed.

WICKERBY

Some say that it was around the time of the Industrial Revolution that we began to go awry, when we instituted the so-called division of labor: men working at machines that make parts for the machines that make ever more parts, thereby severing the worker from the finished work and, thus, from his own soul. Others contend it was many centuries earlier, when the use of the first harnessed plows tore up huge plots of earth and enabled us to feed large numbers of people, who, no longer having to tend to that most basic need, were now free to entertain other needs and invent the technology to satisfy them.

I've heard still others blame the very act of settling itself—of even beginning to tear up, till and irrigate the soil—and suggest as our paradigm the nomadic tribal societies of the Paleolithic age, whose last, withering, vestigial limb Bex and that film crew are out there somewhere in Africa documenting tonight.

Indeed, one popular anarchistic technophobe, whose book I'd been reading in the days before my sudden escape to Wickerby, claims we can begin to put things right again by not only reducing the number of people we bring into the world but by reducing as well the average human's life expectancy to thirty-two years, that being the estimated life span of a Paleolithic tribesman.

"Apprenticed to nature," he declares about the Turkana's distant relatives, "they consciously restricted human numbers and accepted limited human duration, so that other species around them could thrive for the benefit of all."

Taking up my vacuum wand, I pressed on with renewed

vigor about the cabin, essentially drawing lines in the dirt, vacuuming auras around each plate, cup and saucer—my home, I realized, being little more than an act of will, a clearing that I would have to keep making with my hands in the dark. I'd decided to reclaim Wickerby, however briefly, and would take as my cue the industry of the very creatures I was destroying. In them I saw the precedent for myself and for this city that surrounds me again tonight.

I saw it in the relentless borings of the termites, in every web and hapless ensnarement, in all the sidelong hoarding and pilfering. I saw it in the incipient buzz of long-dormant flies and wasps against the newly heated cabin's window-panes; saw it in the frenzy of early-evening bumblebees out by the fire pit, singing past me, loud as mopeds, as though urgently aware of a Canadian summer's brevity. I saw it every night in the swath of reading light above my bed, myriad, nameless things—luminous, diaphanous, winged—swirling, crashing into my book, continuing on: a multi-tiered highway and byway of bugs.

I saw it in the blind persistence of the porcupines who'd apparently concluded that my angry knocks on the floorboards were attempts to communicate and soon had me sitting up at night in eager anticipation of their wire-brush foot massages. I saw it in the mice who'd become so comfortable within whatever faintly repellent vibrations that pest-control device was giving off that they'd often nose their way late at night across the corner oak table as I sat up writing. Settling at the top edge of my notebook, they'd plop back on their haunches and begin nibbling some of the birdseed they'd pilfered from the stash I'd brought for Rasteedy, discarding the empty hulls across my open page.

I saw it in the bats nesting up in the sleeping loft, the bats with whom I would soon effect an unlikely symbiosis indeed. When I first realized, on turning off the reading light one night, that the black-flecked whirring above my bed was, in fact, bats swooping down on mosquitoes, I took to sleeping in the brass bed downstairs in the cabin's southwest corner opposite the oak table and chairs. That bed, however, is positioned right beside a window, and, deciding that it was more essential to my peace of mind to keep at least one floor between myself and all the heart-stopping things that lurk on the other side of dark country windows, I was soon back up in the loft, achieving deep, bug-free sleep just beneath the whir of bat wings.

But I saw it all at once and most clearly as I vacuumed my way to the border of that huge, multistoried carpenter ants' nest in the collapsing southeast corner. It began at the ground in a broad, loosely gathered sprawl of worked earth and wood chips, the structure tapering slightly as it rose into clusters of rooms and tunneled passageways, the entire outside flecked here and there with small, white, windowlike dots—boluses of chewed paper and foam.

A thousand times taller than its builders, it seemed at once enormous and ephemeral, collapsing with each faint flurry of ant feet, giving way to the merest brush of my vacuum, and yet rising ever higher on the spine of the very structure it was displacing, the entire city culminating at a wide, sky-lit breach in the cabin's once-neatly-dovetailed corner, the ants there appearing to move more slowly, as though high atop a mountain, in the ether of less oxygen, even as they continued taking still more of Wickerby up into the next new tier of visitable rooms. And I let them.

A MUMBLER TOLD ME ONCE that sometimes the birds he chases don't come back simply because they travel too far, get so caught up with flying that they go for as long as their wings and wills take them and then have to put over somewhere for the night and start home the following day. Some, he said, don't make it, become disoriented, lose their bearings, and then have to go it alone, hook up with a free flock of "mutts" and start a new life.

I imagine a letter from Bex:

> Dear Charles,
>   I've fallen in love with a nomad. My life
> with you in Brooklyn had become too staid.
> Here I'm always on the move, never in any one

place too long and therefore, strangely, never
afraid, as though our fears accrue in direct pro-
portion to the depth of our belief in the illusion
of permanence, of belonging.
    I must go now. Will explain more later ...

It was mutually exclusive excitement that Bex and I felt when she left here last April. Hers was obvious. She was so taken with the prospect of her adventure, she'd left me days before her actual departure. But there is, too, that vaguely illicit thrill that the one left behind feels, the sense of being suddenly free to explore some long-locked-up room of yourself—a way you seem to remember being before you were bound to someone else. It's a short-lived adventure, I'm afraid, and the exploration a halfhearted one, at once motivated and mocked by the prospect of the true traveler's return.

Down at the street fair now, Wicky Wacky—or is it Wainsy Ranks?—is rapping the night in a syncopated slur of thumps and shouts. Every so often I can see the figure of J, a head taller than his happy fair crowd, passing back and forth, overseeing. Directly below, the man in the house of refuse is sitting on his sofa in the pale lamplight, talking on the telephone. Through my open windows the wasps continue drifting in and out, as though to test the difference between framed air and free, their brief, aimless flights somehow rendering my presence the anomaly.

WICKERBY

On TV, the man in search of noiseless dawns is still standing in a dry riverbed, holding his recorder toward the African sunrise. Lucy is pressed deep into the sofa cushion beside mine, barely raising a brow at the stream of loud barks and growls now coming through my answering machine. This is my friend Frank. He's always leaving Lucy messages. They sometimes go on for minutes. It would only ruin things for him if I were to pick up the phone.

Six floors down, a subway train rumbles past, slightly swaying the Turkana statues. I found them pressed together at the very center of the dresser top when I got back here yesterday, all their wanderings having brought them, in the end, face-to-face, the force of two separate wills forestalling each other's fall. It's something like what the poet Rilke said love should be, the best that it can offer: "that two solitudes protect, border and salute one another," although sitting here tonight, I feel I'm protecting little more than the wounded furnishings of a once-shared life.

"We've just eaten my goat," Bex writes in her most recent letter. "It's raining as it has almost every night despite the drought. I feel very closed in with my tent flaps down, but the rain brings out these horrible creatures called camel spiders, as big as my hand. One of the film assistants says their bite leaves you writhing for a day. As soon as the sun sets they start to swarm. They eat moths and, as moths come to light, you can imagine that I do very little reading or writing here in bed.

"Still, spare time here is so rare that I must put down a little at a time to make sure I have a letter to send when and if I can find someone on their way back to Nairobi. Along with storming through the thorn bushes all day in the hundred-degree heat and dealing with the flies and spiders, there's the constant refrain of packing and unpacking equipment, and then checking everything to be sure it's all right. I'm so tired by the end of the day I'm usually in bed by eight-thirty.

"Our days begin at 4 A.M. We film until noon, return to camp, eat, wash, and set out again until six or seven in the evening. Of course, it's impossible to keep clean. Seconds after a bath, Africa settles back down on you, under your nails, in your hair, up your nose. I can see why the Turkana women never bathe, never from birth. Rather, each morning they coat themselves with ocher. They have a strong scent, like wet, rotting cowhide. Their eyes are deep-set, faces strong. They have great teeth, I suppose from living on a diet of milk.

"I wish I could describe Africa to you, but it is so immense, so beautiful, it often depresses me to try. There is also the feeling that because we're here filming, I am always one step removed from experience. Why am I so happy, then? Often in the day I'll look up and make some passing observation about the land, and having thought it, I'm filled with happiness. Funny to be in a place where the people are so simple and the land the great mystery.

"We moved camp again tonight into this huge wash that over the eons has flooded and dried out. The water has widdled out a swath through the rocks, revealing the striations of time. They are not bands. It's as if the rocks were and are still, viscous, flowing, the lines swirling and diving, thoroughly confusing the ages."

If, for some reason, Bex does not come back; if from our separate wanderings this summer we were to somehow miss each other and continue moving apart, I'll still be able to take as my heart's ransom her Wickerby. Does she even recall, I wonder, the birdhouse that she describes in the diary, building it, she says, when she was ten, and then, with her father, hanging it in the same butternut tree where I would put Rasteedy's cage this spring? Does she know, does she even care to, that the light blue streaks still visible in the cabin's floorboards are, according to Albert, traces of the homemade paint that Wickerby's original builders mixed from blueberries and buttermilk; a mixture which on sun-baked mornings must have given the place the essence of a blueberry muffin?

Perhaps she has little use for such details now. She is difficult to figure when it comes to Wickerby. I remember her violent mood swings during our visit six summers ago, Bex wanting either to get everything back at once, all the details of the one truly happy time she remembers between her parents, or to just abandon Wickerby entirely, let the cabin and its contents rot in place like Miss Havisham's unattended wedding table, and thus become Bex's own little shrine to impermanence, an object lesson about the foolishness of even trusting a commitment enough to furnish it.

Maybe she never had any intention of coming back,

and these past months were part of some elaborate scheme to get away, make a clean break. She dreams up this crazy story about a bare-breast controversy, and leaves her old address book with Wickerby's combination for me to find in her top drawer. Maybe she dispenses with all her men this way, all the ones she's deemed dim enough to require months of trying to resurrect a ruin in order to finally appreciate the fruitlessness of loving her.

I remember telling her one day as we sat by the fire pit that she was behaving a bit like an earthquake victim— afraid to invest her emotions in any one place again, to put valuable objects back up on the shelves. She told me, I believe, to "fuck off." She told me not to dare make her out to be some "poster child of divorce." "Divorce," she said, "happens," and then she stormed away, went, as she would many times during that visit, up to Bex's Rock, a huge ten-foot-high boulder that she discovered as a child in the woods behind Blackberry Field.

I found the rock this spring, would spend many hours up there over the course of my stay. It's the highest point on the land, and Bex said that some days she'd be able to see almost all of Lake Memphremagog from there, stretching twenty-two miles from the town of Newport, Vermont, on the south shore to Magog, Quebec, on the north. The site is entirely engulfed by woods now, but it's still a perfect place to plant yourself in the late afternoon and, like that heron here in the Japanese Garden, let the day pivot around you awhile.

• • •

WICKERBY

There's much I could tell her now about Wickerby, present and past. I've read the diary entries, looked through the photo album. I know that she worried, too, over the bats in the loft; and over the house, "creaking," even back then, "like a ship in a wind storm"; and over the snakes that live in the stone cooking pit. The first fire I made there this spring, they all came wriggling out from the fissures in the rock, baby snakes dropping everywhere into the flames before I could save them.

I know about that tree swallow Bex spotted on the thirtieth of May, 1970, and the catbird she cut free from the latticework of string her father had hung in the garden for his runner beans. I know about the woodpecker she found trapped in the cabin one spring after months away in Montreal. She tried to feed it milk through a ballpoint pen casing, but the bird, "with a great tremor," her father writes on April 9, 1970, "died in Rebecca's hands, and she buried it, crying. We built a cross, inscribed it with the words 'Let nature take its unbending course!'"

I know them all, every plant, creature and star, or I know their avatars, the earth's unbending course yielding to us, the fleeting note-takers, the same, recurring show: the starlings still building their nests in the south-side gables; the snakes sunning themselves along the outer logs of the southeast corner; the woodchuck in the foundation.

"He's back again," Bex's mother writes in a June 6, 1970, entry, "that damn woodchuck, outside the house in the hole beneath the window." I ran, the moment I read this, to the cabin's north-wall shelves and started flipping through the many animal books there, trying to determine the life span of the average woodchuck, wondering if this could possibly be my same woodchuck—one which Bex, a few days after her mother's entry, writes of wanting to make a pet and feed lettuce to even as her father, mindful of his newly planted garden, mused on the very same diary page over the possible ways of killing the animal: "1. Poison 2. Rifle 3. Car exhaust."

That last option I find amusing to contemplate: Bex, age ten, standing disconsolately by while her father, like some crazed cartoon character, hooks up one end of a hose to his car's tailpipe and shoves the other in the nook beneath the cabin, Wickerby's myriad stowaways spilling out, gagging on exhaust, all except for that woodchuck, that indestructible, that by-now-mythical woodchuck.

I have news for Bex of Wickerby—not just of its imminent collapse, but its constancy. I've seen now, too, the dogtooth violets long ago sighted by Bex's uncle just beside the entrance gate. I've seen the horseradish plants, and the pink and white wood violets on the banks of Lake Y-Not, where I played, too, the unwinnable game—or the game that is won in the losing—of trying to outwait a day, of going down to the lake in the evening with a drink, planting my chair in the "boot-eating swamp," as Bex's father called it, and letting the wood's inhabitants come to me. Deer, even a bobcat once. It appeared on the far banks. Took a drink.

There were loons, their laugh-cries hallowing the night. Tanagers, cedar waxwings and evening grosbeaks darted through the dappled light of the shoreline birches. I know them, and know now, as well, the self-indulgent, hypnotic joy of simply sounding all their names again.

WICKERBY

. . .

And if there is a lesson that I was supposed to take from my time at Wickerby, about how easily rich premises can be deserted; about how people can dig gardens and string runner beans and build such solid dormers and memorable days around their secret desire to leave, then I'll take with me as well all the seemingly useless details: the diary accounts of the very day when the electricity first came to Wickerby and the well pump.

I'll take the pictures of Wickerby in the days before there were lights or running water: Coleman lanterns hanging from the rafters and posts; Bex's father, or is it her uncle, what does it matter, chopping through the ice on Lake Y-Not; an old rain barrel set in the grass beside the collapsing southeast corner; the water-can yokes used for the long walks to and from the secret spring in the far back woods.

I'll take, merely to verify the things I just saw, the pictures of the land in long-ago bloom: the simple jonquil, Indian paintbrush and buttercups in the meadow path that winds through Blackberry Field; the tansy, goldenrod, Queen Anne's lace and forget-me-nots in the field behind the stone cooking pit. And I'll take the pictures of the winter that I couldn't hold out to see, Bex's favorite time at Wickerby, she told me, when snow snuffs the surrounding fields and woods into an ashen spray of stems and branches, and the only color for miles is the amber glow of the cabin's lanterns. The diary talks of roast lamb, and there's one picture of Bex, alone on a swinging sofa with a book before a huge Christmas tree.

As for our own diary entries from that visit six summers ago, that's all fixed in my memory anyway. We left from Bex's apartment on the first floor of an old, three-story clapboard house out in Seagate, a private community at the very tip of Coney Island, where she'd moved from Manhattan in the year after her divorce. The place, as I think of it now, was Bex's half-gesture in the direction of Wickerby, a way of leaving the city, just as the mumblers do, without really doing so. At night in her bed, watching the local New York City news, it seemed we were in some faraway, back-country motel room. Just a short walk from her front door, through a swinging metal gate, was the Atlantic Ocean. We'd run Lucy (just a year old then) along the beach, and then climb up the stone breakwater with some beers and our flasks—mine bourbon, hers Irish whiskey (Jameson's, not "lousy Loyalist Bushmills")—and watch the loaded tankers beneath the Verrazano Bridge slide far out to sea.

Bex and I first met at Coney Island, the night that the amusement park's famous Cyclone roller coaster was being officially declared a historic landmark. Bex was covering the event for a Canadian Broadcasting Corporation radio program. I was there with some friends, none of whom would ride the coaster with me.

I hopped into one of the rear cars. Bex was standing close by on the platform in a black sports coat, blue jeans, and a T-shirt, holding her outsized tape recorder microphone to the air, just like the man in search of noiseless dawns, except that she was seeking sound—"ambient sound," she said—jumping into the seat beside mine just as

WICKERBY

I was pulling the latch down. She kept her tape running the entire ride, and now we have for all posterity the recording of our very first meeting: a series of centrifugal screams and grunts.

We left for Wickerby later that summer on a mid-August morning and though we drove more or less straight through, we failed, just as I did this time, to arrive before nightfall. Bex hadn't been to Wickerby in ten years, and as we climbed the entrance road, she was so nervous she could barely get her breath. She would tell me later that her breathing never felt right the whole time we were there.

We made little impression on the place that trip, wandering each day like ghosts through the cobwebbed cabin and the overgrown fields around it, clearing just enough space for ourselves in the dust and droppings to cook our meals and lay our heads down at night to sleep. I did, for a few days, at least, try against all reason and hope to train Lucy, but she'd tear off in excited bursts about the land, stopping back intermittently to look at me with those quizzical tilts of the head, looks that "seemed to ask," Bex wrote in the diary, "'now why is it that we don't live here all the time?'"

The better part of our days—I think to get away from the cabin and all the memories—we spent down at the dock in the nearby town of Georgeville, reading, taking swims in Lake Memphremagog. Bex did bring me to meet Albert one morning and to buy a dozen of his fresh eggs. At fifty cents a dozen—the same price he was asking this summer—they'd be a steal if not for the added cost, also unchanged, of having to listen to his ramblings about the weather or his chores or, his favorite topic, human disaster: car accidents, fires, drownings down in Lake Memphremagog, anything he's heard about from the locals or from his little battery-operated radio. Albert still has no electricity.

Each of his disaster tales he invariably sums up with one of his classic, cryptic pronouncements—"Nooo . . . bud-ahh mean . . . you take life where you can get it . . . Am I righ . . . ?"—and I remember Bex and I standing there in his driveway that morning for over a half hour, nodding and saying yes, again and again, Albert looking the whole time only at me because he's so terribly shy of women, even of Bex, whom he's known since she was three.

Bex says now of that visit to Wickerby that she felt shy there herself the whole time, that she heard too clearly her own shallow breathing. She said Albert's eggs were not as good as she remembered, that the yolks didn't sit as high. One morning, I walked outside the cabin to find her in the field near the top of the entrance road, tugging furiously at a half-buried wagon wheel. She told me there used to be a huge barn on that spot. She and her sisters liked to play in it. She pulled at the wagon wheel again, lost her footing, got up, kicked it and then stormed off, to Bex's Rock, I imagine.

One night, I nearly did lose her for good. She was fiddling with our music box's antenna in the middle of a thunderstorm. The cabin's lightning rod and grounding wire must have absorbed most of the bolt that hit us, but there was enough residual energy to send Bex flying. The antenna still has a sharp bend in it to mark the moment.

The next morning, Bex suddenly declared that it was

time to leave. Before we did, she made us go out and collect kindling. "It's what one does at Wix," she said, "for the next visitor," never thinking then that it would be me. I'm writing it down now, regardless, in the ledgers of impermanence, what good use I made of that kindling, how it fueled my first days and nights at Wickerby.

There's a picture from that first visit. I don't recall who shot it, but if I'm to take anything from these past months, I'm taking that. It's of the north field in the early evening, sunlight slanting late-yellow and low across the black wooden table and two spindled, high-back chairs where Bex and I ate our meals each day at the base of the maple-tree lilac.

I can't decide whether we've just sat there together or are just about to. But I choose to see it now as an extended invitation. The surrounding field and hedgerows, the dark, jagged border of pines against the ongoing sky, all of nature seems to be reappointed, ennobled by our empty place setting: a lightly furnished evening, a way station of air.

OPPOSITE RASTEEDY'S BUTTERNUT, where the top of Wickerby's entrance road crests between a white birch and the last hilltop utility pole—its lone wire limply leashing my days to the outside world—another road starts sharply off to the left, away from the cabin. Leading past an old collapsed stone wall and a tall stand of trembling aspen, it then winds back to the right along the base of Blackberry Field into the woods.

Albert originally carved out the road with his bushwhacker, and still uses it from time to time to collect firewood with his tractor and flatbed trailer. But late nearly every afternoon, when a Wickerby day yawned so wide it seemed to me I'd dissolve if I didn't insinuate myself in some way, this was the path I would take.

By late May, the aspen were covered with silver-backed

leaves, forming a high, mottled, wind-spun wall of light past which Lucy—like some broken-off, suddenly animate section of it—would go bounding. She'd run far ahead through the tall field grass and eventually disappear into the woods, leaving me to follow in behind her.

Just a few steps inside the tree line, I could already feel that dark, cooler, incensed air of a church vestibule. And then, as though I'd left the door open behind me, a huge wind would wash over the upper boughs, leaving me in place, alone, further alone, a feeling I can liken only to my childhood Sundays, that mixture of awe and ennui that ruled the day and could not be outrun.

Names, from then on, can be our only offering. In the beginning, I'd often have with me, like a dutiful worshiper clutching his hymnal, one of the many nature guides Bex's parents had bought over the years and stored on the north-wall shelves: *Native Trees of Canada, Reading the Woods, A Guide to Familiar American Wildflowers, Fiddleheads and Mustard Blossoms: A Guide to Edible Plants of the Forest and Meadow, Stalking the Wild Asparagus, The Book of Ferns, A Field Guide to Mushrooms* and on and on, all remnants of the "back to the land" movement that burgeoned in the 1960s.

I'd pause in the meadow before some lowly, mute, entirely self-absorbed weed, open my book to the page with its approximate (never exact, never satisfyingly certain) representation, and read, as though anointing it right there: "Canada fleabane . . ." Then, as in the church of my youth, I'd read the Latin, "Erigeron canadensis . . . ," followed by the rest of the invocation: "Other names: Horseweed, hog-weed, mare's tail, bitterweed. Habitat: fields, pastures, meadows, gardens, woodland trails, roadsides, waste places . . ."

I'd walk further down the woodland trail, sounding the naturalist's autohypnotic litany: red oak (*Quercus rubra*), white elm—or "elum," as Albert calls them—(*Ulmus Americana*), white birch (*Betuls papyrifera*), trembling aspen (*Populus tremuloides*). I'd go from one to the next, putting each species in its place, pulling a leaf here and there for further examination and identification later in the cabin. And then one day I just stopped bothering, found myself to be much less concerned with names than I was with the awful isolation of being the only one out there wielding them.

"The path of things is silent," wrote Emerson. I was not surprised to find an old collection of his essays on the north-wall shelves. "Will they suffer a speaker to go with them. A spy they will not suffer; . . . The condition of true naming . . . is resigning yourself to the divine aura which breathes through forms, and accompanying that."

This would soon become another of my favorite enterprises at Wickerby: playing that impossible game of trying not to think. I'd walk into the woods and try instead to let all of my thoughts unravel into the surrounding thoughtlessness and then accompany it—a deep silence that, by isolating the sound of our thoughts and words, and the very impulse to create them, threatens, the longer it lasts, to expel us from our very being.

I would go into the woods at Wickerby precisely to feel this expulsion, to feel what we all feel in the woods but don't like to admit to: cast out by them, the most firm and yet pure rebuke that we'll ever receive. No buildings, no windows, no human framework, just me and my fellow DNA assemblages—the trees and birds, the ferns, mosses, mushrooms, worms, mites and myriad invisible things—all blankly thriving there around me: the wide accident, the inherent anonymity of existence.

The path forks about a mile in. To the right, down a gently sloping hill, it leads, after another mile or so, to a low, swampy expanse—what Bex and I had dubbed "the great tree burial ground" when we first came upon it six summers ago. The rising water table there has uprooted and toppled a number of giant oaks, birches and spruce, leaving a wide opening in the forest canopy above.

There always seems to be a mist in that hollow, and this summer I liked to walk into it, climb up onto one of those felled giants and, pressing back against their unforgiving bulk, take the full measure of my slightness. I'd just lie there in silence, daring to linger in an unappointed, nameless present. I'd wait until I couldn't stand it any longer—dizzying, nearly noxious spells of self-abnegation.

Other days, I'd take the left fork, up a steep incline, to the very eastern edge of Wickerby's land and the site of Bex's Rock. With the old hilltop view obstructed now by the trees, there is little to do anymore but sit back and absorb the surrounding commerce—existence, chasing down, without reflection, its various needs—and me just holding there, in silence, feeling at once a part of and apart from everything.

WICKERBY

I'd hold on as long as I could, as though by doing so, by fully accompanying things, some previously unseen trap door might suddenly open and readmit me into what, I now understand, none of us were ever expelled from to begin with; readmit me into the very place that I already occupied there up on Bex's Rock, and that I occupy here tonight.

I'm putting it down now in the Wickerby diary, how the moments that I'll remember best from my stay there are the ones I could least inhabit, moments when I felt the full expanse of the apparent divide between myself and those woods; when I felt most deeply that disappointment that overcame me the first day I stepped outside the cabin door, a disappointment not in but from my surroundings, a sense of exile that is, in the end, coincidental with consciousness.

It's a disappointment that we perhaps feel more deeply today than ever before, rooted as it is in the disparity between the ways in which our various machines can now re-create and represent the world, and the way that the world, unattended, unedited, just lies there; the disparity between this flitting, narrated, nature-show night in which the man in search of noiseless, unadorned dawns regales me with one well-framed sunrise after the next, and the sunrise it-self; between the film being made of the Turkana's world, and the world as it falls tonight before their eyes out on the African plains.

I'd wait up there on Bex's Rock, poised on the verge of pure thoughtlessness, of full accompaniment; poised, exactly like that heron in the Japanese Garden atop the pond's NO FISHING sign—motionless, reflectionless—but for one slight catch that has now made what seems to be a world of difference between ourselves and other beings; one snag in the arrangement of our DNA strands that strands us from all the others, that made our minds' biological matter rove over into consciousness which traps, like a sluice gate, what otherwise flows uninterrupted through the heron's and all other creatures' eyes; traps all the objects and occurrences which, named and recognized, both frame and inform the otherwise seamless squares of light and breath that we call days.

I'm putting it down now, some account of the hours I spent up there on Bex's Rock, accompanying things, trying, in a sense, to devolve backward toward some imagined convergence with the woods around me, only to repeatedly confront that one little catch, that snag—call it consciousness, recognition, whatever—that makes us the only ones who long to be a part again of that to which we already belong. The catch that makes us think of ourselves as the outcasts, the unnatural ones, and that first compelled us to conceive of a story like that of Adam and Eve, who took the fruit of a forbidden knowledge that was already ours to begin with. It's the snag, the spur, the one genomic gaff that explains how the original descriptions of the very garden paradise from which we were supposedly cast out could, in fact, have been inspired by the sight of a city in the first place: desert-wandering Hebrew tribes suddenly coming upon the plush gardens growing inside the walls of Byzantium.

I went day after day into the deep silence of those woods only to learn why it is that we, ultimately, can't stand a stand of trees; why we are, in fact, impelled by the woods to leave them and then to try to reconfigure the awe that we felt there in the form of this city that I've come home to tonight, this steepled awe.

I went into the woods at Wickerby precisely to feel that one difference, the one chance nudge of our nucleotides within evolution's ongoing chain of aminos that has made us the only creatures who, in the end, prefer to the actual place, the show: this city's walled stay against wilderness with its own built-in, visitable squares of that wilderness as well, whether it's Olmsted and Vaux's appointed woods, or the Botanic Garden's numbered paths, or this flashing TV square wherein the man goes on in search of noiseless dawns, or the fenced-off rhinoceros in the zoo down the block.

He used to be—if you entered the zoo's side gate behind Prospect Park's century-old, wooden carousel, and then walked up a brief hill—your very first encounter, standing there on his small, grassless patch of Brooklyn the way rhinos everywhere and for millennia have stood: two small eyes peering out of dirt-caked armor, the horned head heavily drifting an inch or so above the earth.

Rudy was there as far back as the late 1950s, when my father was first bringing me with him to this neighborhood on his so-called weekend cultural outings from Flatlands. Along with the zoo, these would typically entail a stroll through the Botanic Gardens, lunch over at the museum, with perhaps a quick visit to the Egyptian mummies or to

Colonel Milligan's and all the other period rooms. My father—a machinist, a "tool-and-die" man, who spent the better part of his life selling random electrical parts for TVs and phonographs: phono jacks, alligator clips and circuit boards—always preferred the functional and historical to the abstract. After the museum, the highlight of the day for my father, and, if you ask me, the pretext for the entire venture, would be a ball game at Ebbets Field.

Still, the outings did continue long after this last part of the day was eclipsed by the Dodgers' sudden departure for the West Coast in 1957, when I was just three. I remember nothing of the ball games now except for one night, running my toy truck along the railing of the box seat directly in front of mine, wondering whether the rhinoceros could hear the roar of the crowd in his small, fur-tipped ears.

Rudy was never a very big draw, being, I suppose, entirely too unanimated, too much of what he was, to look at for very long. And yet, like the shore of Lake Y-Not, or the woods around Bex's Rock, I found him more enticing to draw near to for that: a stillness to be outmatched by, a breathing part of prehistory, sensate stone.

I'd stand at the edge of his sunken, walled enclosure, waving, making noises, trying to take the measure of his ken: whether he ever swayed with the carousel's spin; if sudden police sirens startled him; if he even blinked at the sparrow's chirps or the starling's squeaks, and if he recognized the difference between those and the songs of African birds like his age-old, symbiotic sidekick the oxpecker, who hitches rides upon his bristle-plated back in exchange for plucking off all the mites and parasites.

WICKERBY

The day I moved here ten years ago, I walked down to the zoo to see if Rudy was still there. It's not often that a Brooklynite can claim a rhinoceros as a contemporary. Once Bex settled in with me, it became a regular part of our afternoon walks with Lucy through the park to stop by and pay Rudy a visit. Dogs aren't allowed into the zoo, but a short way up from the side entrance, along a low stone wall that skirts the zoo's outmost, barred perimeter, we found a spot where we could see directly into Rudy's plot.

Lucy would prop her front paws on top of the wall, her pinhead just able to see over. She'd emit these tentative, low idling-engine growls that Rudy seemed never to hear or care much about. And then one afternoon this past winter, he actually swayed his huge head in our direction and locked eyes with Lucy: a stare-down that I would eventually have to interrupt because the vortex of thoughtlessness gathering there between those two seemed about to swallow up all of Brooklyn.

I went back down to the zoo this morning before the start of the fair, walked along Washington Avenue across Eastern Parkway—the refilled and now, dare I say it, nearly completed parkway—passing the museum and the Botanic Gardens, entering Prospect Park through the domed granite portals of Willink Gate. The zoo's side entrance is just off to the right, behind the carousel, already going when I arrived, children clutching their wild-eyed steeds and dragons as that slow, sad calliope filled the morning air.

A chain-link fence now blocks the zoo's old iron-barred entrance, a sign posted there explaining that the place is being converted into "a cageless natural habitat," an interactive facility where visitors will be able to roam freely among wallabies and pheasant, gray geese and prairie dogs—a kind of mini–fearless forest.

Looking in through the barred gate, I could see down the main walkway toward the old zoo center, built back in 1935, the now-stagnant seal pool set inside a semicircle of granite, Beaux Arts animal houses with their action reliefs up along the frieze, and, gracing the front entranceways, proud statues of the animals housed within. All was intact, and eerily silent, like a suddenly abandoned city, dead leaves blowing across the cobblestone walks, and the animal houses' outdoor cages, swirling through those little metal trapdoors in the back wall between daylight and phosphorescence.

There is an odd innocence about old city zoos, monuments at once to our complete awe and ignorance of the animals. Somehow, it was enough for us just to get them here, to give them a room of their own with an outdoor patio option, and, inside, a chained log, perhaps, or a few rocks, or a rope swing as a token acknowledgment of their original home.

We'd step inside the Ape House, into that odor and the anomaly of our own harshly lit, echoing voices. Then we'd proceed to take in the exhibits. No details about them or their world to mitigate our experience, just a metal nameplate with GORILLA, the Latin below it, and a dot on a silhouette of Africa. And there, sitting in a yellow-tiled room like a subway-station toilet, was the gorilla, looking at once larger than life and yet, given the accommodations, greatly reduced by it, like some guy who just got a bad evolutionary break.

Just before the Ape House exit there was that last set of bars with the big, undulant, fun-house mirror behind them and the words "The Most Dangerous Animal of All!" painted below. Everyone would stop in front of it and laugh and then step back outside for a moment into the city daylight before entering the Lion House. Or they'd walk over to watch the seals, their quicksilver, body-long presses through water somehow serving as captivity's antidote. I remember as a child being made to wait there by the seal pool railing while my father went to use the men's room, located beneath the Lion House, the image of him descending the stone stairway into a darkness of caged roars.

Looking to the right of the zoo's main walkway, I could see into all the deserted bear dens—Polar, Brown, Grizzly, Asiatic—set side by side against a common back wall of steep, rough-hewn glacial rock, the moats up front all drained now, ribbed with the shadows of their high, curved-tip bars. I found myself checking the polar bear's den for any sign of the events of last spring—a torn shred of clothing, perhaps, bloodstains—but saw nothing.

Far to my left, the old eagle, hawk and vulture cages—cartoonish, outsized versions of the gilded Victorian models in Colonel Milligan's library—were stacked together in a thicket of park trees, starlings and sparrows flitting in and out of the open doors. Just in front of them were the empty, weed-strewn enclosures in which the llamas, zebras and giraffes used to be kept. To my immediate left, in a grouping more circus-mined than zoological, was the sunken, iron-railinged roundlet of evolution's thick-skinned, rotund odd-ities: the elephants, the hippos and Rudy.

He's no better off in Michigan. He probably hates the sub-urbs, standing out there on some distant, moated island of habitat grass, people sliding by overhead, waving like dis-missive gods from the monorail. Once he'd suffered the ini-tial insult, who's to say he hadn't grown to like it here in Brooklyn with the so-called family of man, the daily blurred and squawking outline of us on the periphery of his nearsightedness.

I'm the last person who should begrudge an already-endangered species a reprieve from this neighborhood, but then why does the zoo down the block get dismantled just because the animal's home in the wild has been? Why bring animals all this way just to place them too far away to see? Why not refurbish the old place for the old residents, like they're doing with our parkway, and then, as they now do in Japanese zoos, give Rudy and the others assigned, up-close viewing hours after which the animals get the rest of the day off?

They belong here beside us anyway, have earned that right by now. They belong if only for the way that Rudy's presence at the corner of Flatbush and Ocean Avenue seemed to throw the whole proposition of us and our cities into question. This, for all its crudeness, was the strangely affecting dynamic of the old city zoo. While a visit there may have begun with us standing starkly, face-to-face, with a captured and compromised creature, it always seemed to end with us confronting a deeply confining truth about ourselves. There's an initial sense of exhilaration that allows us to forget the overpowering of the animals that was re-uired to represent its power again, and then an incipient sadness that grows out of that moment and fills us with a vague measure of gloom about our need to spy on animals in the first place, about that one catch, squiggle, snag that makes us the only creatures who need to look at all the others and give them names, to stare at them and wonder what they might be thinking; the only ones who need to piggyback on them for our own edification and yet give nothing in return.

It isn't in us to let them just be animals, to let them be. They must represent something, even these last, zoo-bound few. They represent, we believe, "Nature," these select few that we've been loading all along into Colonel Milligan's Ark to take with us against what we believe to be the all-consuming tide of us, when, in fact, our ship and all of its passengers—we and all the other large, land-based animals—occupy but one brief wave swell of living matter, constitute little more than the spume above the wave of moiling DNA tides below.

Call them what we will—arks, zoos, habitats, wilder-ness parks—it was never about the animals anyway. We don't really go to zoos to learn about them. We go to have some telling turn with evolution's otherness, to look at the ways we didn't end up being, all the shapes that a nonreflective will can take. We are such lonely, fleeting observers of evolution's slow-moving work that somehow going to a zoo and staring at animals can stay us awhile, reinvolve us in the matter of existence.

Rudy's no better off in Michigan. He's where we can feel better about our continued need to keep him. He's where we've been trying to get him and the others all along: into the suburbs of our affections, retirement homes for the wild, deftly rendered wilderness dioramas that at once try to conceal from the animals their captivity and from ourselves that one catch, that squiggle, that snag that compels us to be their keepers.

I visited the newly renovated, habitat-oriented Bronx Zoo one day last winter. At their old zoo center, an area known as Astor Court, a series of signs was strung along the outer cages of the now-abandoned Lion and Ape Houses: ANIMALS ARE NOT HOME. GONE NATURAL. . . . LIVING IN WILD HABITATS.

Above me, through the pale light of Astor Court, visitors slipped by on a monorail. I followed beneath them, along a stone footpath, eventually arriving at "Wild Africa": a wide-open expanse of tree-dotted plain where gazelles and peacocks drifted around a moated, inner island of lions lazing in the grass.

I remember being briefly taken in by the scene, and then a pigeon flew by, drawing my eye to some local city shrubbery, then to an oak tree where a squirrel scampered up a limb and unseen starlings squeaked. And it was at this near-seamless juncture of the habitat's evoked nature and the city's local patch of it that the two worlds blurred, and it occurred to me that for us the "wild" has only ever been an idea: something we flee if it's too close, or romanticize if too remote. The only viable meeting place that civilization has been able to negotiate between the absence and presence of the wild is the zoo.

I often think of Rudy now, standing out there on that night last spring when those kids climbed into the polar bears' moat. I wonder if their screams and then the shotguns lifted, even briefly, his hooded lids, before everything settled down again into a soft, tensile urban silence, leaving the pall with us, the confusion and the questions, only with us: What were those kids thinking, and how could they have gotten in, and why didn't the police have tranquilizer guns? Why did they have to kill the bears, the true innocents in the whole affair?

I think of Rudy, of all the animals, think of the other bears right next door, asleep that evening, I imagine, in their carved, back-wall caves when they were drawn out by the screams. I see the big cats over in the Lion House, stirring, and the already stir-crazy jaguar that pads all day in his cell, padding faster; and the gorillas, waking from their torpor, casting deep, slow, over-the-shoulder gazes in the direction of the screams just as all the seals at the pool outside plunged down off their rookery in search of a deeper darkness.

Can we arrest any further, I wonder, the already arrested, the innocents, the ones that we still can't let just be the animals? "It was very hot," said the boy who did climb back out in time, "and we wanted to take a swim." But I realize now that when they climbed into the polar bears' den that night, they were climbing into the story of the bears, the idea, the aura of them, into all that polar bears represent. Kids here on hot nights will run through park sprinklers, attach hoses to spigots, pull caps off hydrants, anything to escape the heat, and if they sneak into a zoo, there are any number of less threatening pools— the seals' for one—in which to cool off. These boys, how- ever, sought out the polar bears' moat—not the coldest pool, but the pool of the animal that represents coldness: the ice bears of TV nature shows and of children's books; the bears who ride blocks of ice across soda-bottle labels and menthol cigarette packs.

It was a hot night, and the boys climbed into the ice bears' moat, and then came the screams, and people's faces to the lighted windows above, and a web of phone calls and sirens, and then the shotguns, the percussive blasts knocking, I imagine, the caged birds off their perches, making the llamas lurch, and the massive heart of the giraffe miss a beat, forcing its high-perched brain to feed that much longer off the little carburetor sponge of blood at the back of its skull—the blood that keeps the light rolling behind the giraffe's eyes, behind all the animals' eyes, through which whole days pass uninterrupted.

No catch for them, no snag, no storied aftermath to contemplate, neither from that night nor from past nights; no echoes heard in all that bear-den tumult of our past assaults upon them, of the long centuries of capture. No footsteps of the earliest animal-gathering expeditions,

Egyptian queens and Chinese emperors sending ships across the seas to collect creatures for their private zoos. No ghosts of Alexander the Great's animal-gathering brigade, nor of the Romans capturing all of Europe's lions and bison and wolves for their huge, artificial amphitheater forests, wherein animals and citizens would be turned loose for a day's hunt. No echoes in the boys' screams and the subsequent slaughter of that one day in the reign of Julius Caesar, in which six hundred lions and twenty elephants were slain.

Nothing. Just another night last spring in their cages, and then the silence broken by the stealthy tiptoe of the boys' sneaking past them, much like that night in 1789, I'm imagining now, when a desperate mob crept into Louis XVI's Menagerie Royale. The animals they didn't eat were donated to the formation of the first public city zoo at Paris's Jardin des Plantes. Six years later, the first known study of animal sensitivity was conducted there, the first real attempt to get to know them. A full orchestra played to an elephant. It reportedly swayed to marching music and slept through a symphony.

The boys tiptoed past the cages, climbed up and over into the bears' moat, and then came the screams and the guns and the terror rippling, as though across a still pond's surface, through all the animals' eyes and down into their hearts. Screams and then the shots ringing out, pinging through the bars and the railings and the animal house tiles; all the animals' heads turning at once and the tremors running inward and then back out toward the tips of their claws as the dead boy and bears were taken away and the gates reclosed, and then that silence, settling, without reflection, over everything, leaving only the pall and the questions with us.

I imagine Rudy, holding there to his plot, trembling, beneath these same steep buildings and stunted stars, and then, hours later, beneath the same sound that comes over the city late each night—a sound that has followed me all my life—of someone flying alone in a single-engine plane, the long drone, diminishing, over distant, lake-folds of air. I remember as a child out in Flatlands, lying awake long after my father had shut out the light, listening for that sound, a low, rumbling growl like that of a caged, slow-padding jaguar, Rudy slowly resettling beneath his hooded lids, blinking back the surrounding building lights on his way to sleep and whatever it is that a displaced rhinoceros dreams.

Down at the fair, the music has stopped. The pigeons—as though the entire city just flinched—fly briefly up, then resettle on their sills. There's a thump on the microphone. J is introducing the next performer, the evening's featured guest, "Desert Sax," a neighborhood kid, an ex-Marine, seen across the nation on the nightly news a few years back playing his saxophone in the dunes of Kuwait during the Persian Gulf War. "He's a lot safer over there," J used to tell me.

Above the ripening bricks and cement now, high sax notes scatter the day's last starlings toward the dwindling light. I want this hour to keep arriving, the way I used to imagine it through that mumbler's eyes when he'd come back down to his window each evening: the rush of light and desire all pivoting around that inner core of repose gathered from a prolonged visit with the very blankness that first disposed us to build all this.

It's the most we can ask for, I think, the noted passing of a gathered repose. I'm putting it down here now: my time at Wickerby as a tale of lost accompaniment. It's much like the story I found in the cabin one night in an old copy of *Alice in Wonderland,* Bex's name in childish scrawl across the inside cover.

At one point in the course of her journey on the far side of the looking glass, Alice comes upon a cool, shady wood "where things have no names." Immediately upon entering, she forgets what to call the very tree under which she's standing, and entirely forgets what to call herself. She next comes face-to-face with a fawn, which, not being recalled by Alice as such, is completely fearless and walks farther through the woods, side by side with her, in a spell of peace and calm. But after a time, the two emerge back out into an open field, whereupon name recognition suddenly returns and the fawn breaks free and bounds away, leaving Alice "almost ready to cry with vexation at having lost her fellow traveler so suddenly."

I would stay up there sometimes on Bex's Rock, without appointment or names, until the sky began to darken and a deep, sourceless dread came over me. I'd wait there until all that was left of me was a faint inner voice, marking the depths of aimlessness through which I was falling, and then, by the thin strains of that voice, I'd pull myself up and start home.

I'd walk down through the woods and out into Blackberry Field, the cabin's slanted roof coming into view, swaying, with each of my steps, atop the trees. I'd follow the path along the base of the field to the high row of aspen, and then turn, Wickerby settling down stoutly again into the tall grass before me—the very first house, the only house in the world.

BY THE TIME SUMMER arrived at Wickerby, I had settled into a fairly solid if rather unremarkable routine there. Having collected on all my sleep debts, I soon found myself getting up each day at around eight A.M., which left me a full morning for writing. After lunch I'd read by the window with the plum tree branches and then do some work in the pathetic little vegetable garden, which, without any good idea of what I was doing, I suddenly decided to dig one day in early May along the road beyond the butternut tree. Late afternoons, after a swim in Lake Y-Not, I'd go for my walk, collecting kindling on the way home for the evening fire.

This was the part of my day—lighting the fire in the stone cooking pit and then sitting beside it with a drink— that I most savored, the point at which, having spent so much time alone with my thoughts, I wanted nothing more than to set them all alight with a couple of bourbons, my brain and the fire pit's logs in mutual conflagration, a notebook always kept in my shirt pocket to capture the occasional spark flying up before me.

I don't know the specific biology, how many brain cells one can use for kindling in a lifetime before the whole pile gets depleted. But insofar as writing, and living for that matter, are for me limiting enterprises, by which every choice made precludes too many others, I find that a few strong early-evening bourbons have a way of blowing open whatever trap it is that I've construed for myself by day's end, allowing me at least a brief review, past the flying, incendiary wreckage, of the roads not taken.

This process in itself requires a good deal of vigilance, as alcohol readily blurs that line between the noteworthy and the nonsensical. At Wickerby, I usually found that sound, reliable judgment lasted well into the second bourbon—which, perhaps because of the relative vigor and salubriousness of a country day, is a good sight longer than it lasts with my urban bourbons—and then I'd just leave off note-taking, stoke the fire and get quietly soused.

Summer evenings at Wickerby, there is a moment when the wind suddenly dies—you can practically hear a switch being flipped offstage—and then nothing stirs across the hilltop. This was when Bex and I would play a good rousing round of Tenn-Bad, the game we invented from the available implements in the cabin's junk corner. It's essentially badminton but with tennis rackets and no net. Or it's tennis but played under twenty feet of water: the air-thickened flight of the shuttlecock affording the exquisite experience of being able to swing full force and yet play in artful slow motion.

I tried in Bex's absence to invent a game of Tenn-Bad fetch with Lucy one spring evening, but quickly learned that her taste for birdies extends to the inanimate variety as well. Shy a viable playing partner, I'd pass the hours before dinner sitting with Lucy by the fire pit, listening to the evening news on the radio, staring out eastward across the valley to the upward-sloping fields of Albert's farm, his cattle having moved by then high up along the back pasture fence, trying to capture the day's last light against their flanks as though riding on some unseen seesaw with the setting sun.

Upon my arrival at Wickerby this spring, I only knew about Albert, our one previous meeting aside, what I'd been told by Bex or had managed to read in the Wickerby diaries over the course of my first few nights. Bex said he didn't own his land or house, that they are leased to him for next to nothing by a wealthy local Hereford breeder with ties to Albert's family, the Shaws, one of the many Scottish immigrant families who first settled in the area around the time of the Revolutionary War. Albert was born and raised just outside the nearby town of Fitch Bay. In his mid-sixties now, he's lived by himself there across the valley from Wickerby for close to forty years. He does have a number of brothers and sisters, but none of them— according to Byron Elliot, a local farmer who stopped by

Wickerby one morning unannounced—live in the area any longer.

"Byron Elliot!" he shouted, a gentle, jowly, ovoid figure half-jogging toward me in overalls, his hand held out, his station wagon left running at the top of the entrance road, its front door wide open. This, I would be repeatedly reminded over the coming months, is the way of the country. It seems the more space there is between people, the more brazen they are about bridging it, whereas one of the abiding charms of the city is the way people's close proximity to one another begets their complete distance and estrangement.

"Byron Elliot . . ." he said again as we shook hands. "Like the poet."

"Which one?" I asked, thinking myself quite clever until he rejoindered, and in a tone that indicated he'd had to do so hundreds of times before, "Mr. Thomas Stearns Eliot spelled his name with one *l*. Mine has two."

In the course of Mr. Elliot's impromptu visit—which, it turned out, had an ulterior motive: a rather offbeat request for a clipping from the old apple tree that stands in Wickerby's north field just beyond the lilac-rimmed sugar maple—I would also learn that one of Albert's brothers is a college professor, in Toronto, that one of his sisters "is a real beauty," and that while Albert sometimes seems a little off, no one can say what exactly is wrong with him.

"He's got a hell of a lot more on the ball than you might think," Byron told me.

As for what Albert made of me and my sudden arrival at Wickerby, I can only imagine, although I was pretty sure he'd determined that there wasn't any real purpose in my being there, or, at least, not one for which he had much sympathy or use. I wasn't farming, I wasn't hunting or logging and I wasn't repairing the cabin in any substantive way.

Albert would surely have known if I were. Years of lonely silence have honed his senses. He knew everything: what I did all day, all my comings and goings, and what I had in the car with me. Little conversational asides within the course of the protracted aside that is any conversation with Albert would expose his uncanny vigilance: ". . . when you went into town for your groceries yesterday . . ." he'd say, or ". . . bout the time you started your fire in the woodstove this morning . . ."

In the evenings, the valley between his hillside and mine formed a huge sound trough that would collect the slightest offering, hold it up on the air for you: the last engine snarl of an overworked tractor; the dull bone-spank of wood being stacked three farms away; high-pitched, distant voices in broken, flyaway pieces. Even when Albert was in his house at the end of a workday, I could sense his presence down there, watching and listening from behind his blanketed windows.

My first encounters with him this spring were all on his terrain, or, I should say, with it. Albert wears the earth. It's rubbed deep into his polyester, hand-me-down clothes, much like those worn by the Indians I'd visited in the Amazon—double-knit pants and flowered shirts and patent-leather, brown loafers with gold-plated buckles on the instep. It's packed beneath his fingernails, wedged into the folds of his inner elbows, and the creases of his sunburnt neck, and the crow's-feet of his eyes. Bex said to me once that Albert's smell was always her favorite thing about him, kind of a slow-baked, sweat-tinged clay.

I'd stop by just to ask him questions about the cabin or buy some of his eggs, Bex having made it quite clear to me that buying Albert's eggs, whether I planned to eat them or not, was a Wix tradition and a necessary courtesy. Every week I'd walk down Wickerby's long, hillside entrance road, cross the main dirt road running through the base of the valley between Albert's place and mine, and then head up the dusty drive that leads around to his back door.

It's the only door Albert uses anymore, his boarded-up front entrance and undulant wood porch barely visible now behind a tall, dense thicket of sumac. The whole house sags, a weathered, single-framed affair propped up here and there on stone and cinder block, the outside of the house a hodgepodge of sidings: plywood, shingles and masonry board. Bex swears that underneath it all there's a log cabin just like Wickerby.

A squat, tin-roofed areaway juts off the back of the house, with a two-tiered wooden door, the slight shelf along the lower half giving the place the look of a small, back-country store. I found the top half open the first time I approached and, blocking the sunlight from my eyes, called into the darkness. The outline of Albert's spare furnishings slowly came into focus: the front of a metal sink and a white stove in the kitchen area just inside the shanty, and then further on, within what looked like his main living quarters, a sofa bed pushed up under one of the blanketed front windows, and a small nightstand beside the bed with an old radio on it.

Albert's inbred, cross-eyed, six-toed cats circled at my feet. Inside, I heard the door to a woodstove clank shut and then Albert's lean figure shuffling forward, two hands pressing a cap to his mostly bald head. He had on the same grease- and dirt-smeared polyester dress shirt and double-knit pants cinched with a knotted belt high above his waist; and the same oversized and cracked brown patent-leather loafers with the gold-plated buckles.

"What's a matter . . . house fall on your head?" he asked, his voice a high, flat, pinched thing, always trailing off into flinty snickers over his own jokes.

"Have any eggs, Albert?"

"Yeah, got some," he said, barely audibly, disappointed that I hadn't entertained his question.

"House fall down yet?" he insisted.

"Gonna go any day," I shouted back, purposely echoing Albert's own refrain to him as he headed up the hill toward the chicken barn, holding one of the empty cartons he keeps around for occasional patrons like me. Moments later, he came back with a dozen eggs. I handed him two quarters. Silence.

"Have a bad winter?" I asked.

"Terrible," he said, tracing a quick outward arc with his finger, directing my eye to the forest along the back edges of the farm pastures around us, all the tree trunks bare to the same height, like the hem of a very short skirt.

"Deer ate as far up as they could reach," Albert said, waving his hand to indicate he'd had enough of this subject.

I made some reference to Wickerby creaking in the storm of a few nights before, told him how I could hear the windowpanes in the southeast corner cracking, all so that Albert could go into his cabin spiel. He did, for a good ten minutes or so. Then I thanked him for the eggs and started away.

"She here with you?" he called out. It took me a second to realize that he meant Bex.

"No," I said, "she's in Africa."

"What she doin there? Eating monkeys?" Giggles and bobs and weaves. He then went on to tell me everything he knew about people eating monkeys and other unimaginable things—grasshoppers, ants, snakes, dogs, cats and on and on. He'd heard all about it on his radio.

"Probably," I said. "She loves monkey . . ." and that sent him back into the house, extremely happy.

Over time, our exchanges would become more relaxed, and Albert was soon inviting himself up the road for his regular cabin lecture-tours. Somewhere along the line, he seemed to have decided—perhaps by virtue of my size alone, which at six feet and 210 pounds made his 140 pounds stretched over the same height seem particularly scrawny—that despite my nearly complete detachment from the world of manual labor, I was substantive enough, man enough, to be taken seriously.

WICKERBY

At least, more so than Bex's uncle Michael, let's say, Wickerby's part-owner, a world-renowned James Joyce scholar and an expert gardener who, as far as Albert is concerned, should be known only as the useless nincompoop who wouldn't know a hammer from a wrench; who planted the trees too close to the cabin's foundation; and who, because he didn't have the common sense to drain the water from Wickerby's newly installed porcelain toilet before closing up the cabin one winter many years ago, cracked the bowl in two when he sat upon it the following spring—a story that all these years later still sends Albert into writhing, soundless, gum-agape laughter every time he tells it.

I, in turn, would vastly overplay my delight in such tales, both to assert my manliness and to keep on Albert's good side, on the off chance that I'd need his assistance sometime over the course of my stay. The more immediate and dubious dividend, however, was that Albert soon began to feel more comfortable about coming up the road to see me, sometimes two and three times a week, often enough, in fact, to indicate that he'd become as curious about me and the idle, abstract nature of my workdays as I'd been about the active, tactile tenor of his.

In my car one morning, I passed him walking along the main dirt road a mile or so from his house, and drove him the remaining distance to the old gray toolshed that the farmer up the way lets Albert use to repair his equipment. Albert hopped out and swung open the shed's wide wooden door. Behind it was his red International Harvester tractor, circa 1955, with its small mismatched front tires and its badly chipped, deep-treaded rear ones, nearly as tall as I.

He went right to work. "Busted generator," he mumbled, shuffling back and forth between the greased inner shadows of the garage's shelved parts and the tractor engine's reticular, sunlit assemblage of them. I stood by, observing his work, his utter fluency in the inscrutable dialect of machines, feeling, for all of my size over him, weightless, a mere gnat on the periphery of his day.

This was when I decided to dig my garden. Here I am, I thought, the son of a former tool-and-die worker, standing idly by on the outskirts of work; another a-manual, postmodern meta-man of the fully automated, computer-driven world, standing there, twiddling my increasingly unopposed opposable thumbs, regarding my own disengaged, physically disappointed self.

I remembered then an air-traffic controller I'd read about years ago, a man so frazzled by the daily, frenzied shepherding of those abstract flashes across his computer radar screen—each flash a planeload of humanity—that he finally decided to build a ship with his own hands, frame first, the way the Greeks built them, the skeleton of the idea, then the flesh, each board soaked in salt water, conditioned to its destiny, shaped to the keel, and then he climbed aboard and slowly sailed himself back to sanity.

Dig a garden, I told myself, and don't fall into the trap of mistaking your own cranky, aging idleness for that imaginary condition known as the increased speed of modern life. Dig a garden. That will reacquaint you with your discomfited bulk right quick. *It* isn't going any faster these days, and it certainly isn't going anywhere. We are not, no matter how many hours we might stare at flashing com-

WICKERBY

puter screens, visiting virtual realities, about to sidestep this present one. We are not—although the urge to do so is as old as consciousness—about to download our bodies, shed this "mortal coil," gather ourselves "into the artifice of eternity," or cyberspace, as it's currently called.

We all find refuges from the flash and flurry of our mechanisms. We turn them off and then drag our disengaged selves out for a walk or a run, make them lift weights, build a fence, a house, go work in the yard, dig a garden. The modern mind can spin more than one plate. People can absorb in the same day both a hyper- and a real text; can have both virtual and real sex in the same day. My hand, this human hand, might with one touch of a button initiate a whole series of synaptic, unseen, electronic events, and still want the fever rush of human touch. The one, just because it's newly invented, does not, as is so often assumed, displace the desire for the other.

And neither have my days at Wickerby—the ongoing absence of buildings and appointments—ill disposed me to these Brooklyn days, or pointed up to me, by contrast, the intolerable pace of modern life. I sped home yesterday from the gradualness of Wickerby at seventy miles an hour, only to deliver myself to this hesitant hour, couched here amidst all the outward hurry and clamor, my heart quickened now by the thought of a call from Bex, and then slowed again by the touch of my hand upon Lucy's flank, and then both quickened and slowed with each long look out my window at the gathering splendor of another city night.

Dig a garden, I thought, if for no other reason than to forget yourself for a while.

Albert, for his part, hardly ever spoke of himself. A simple question about his health, and he'd go all funny and quiet, look down at the ground, take his cap off, rub his baby-bald-eagle head and mutter with his face moving away: "Yeah, m'allright." If he did offer up a rare bit of self-analysis, it would not be about his frame of mind, but some malfunctioning aspect of his aging, overworked frame.

"Arm don't work like it used to," he suddenly announced that day outside the maintenance shed, as though he were a mere extension of the motor he was fixing.

"Fella up the road here . . ." he continued, hopping into the bare, burnished metal tractor seat. It looked like an oversized catcher's mitt. "He died this winter. Just forty-three years old. Bad pump. But that's what ahm sayin. You take life where you can. Know whad ahm sayin? Am I righ?" He started up the tractor engine, got down, put away his tools, then came back into the sunlight, squinting. "Nooo . . . bud . . . ayh mean . . . that's how life is. You don't die till you get around to it."

When Albert first started coming up the Wickerby road in the evenings, he wouldn't venture far from his tractor. Sometimes he'd come up and keep going, mowing the land without my having asked him to. He'd buzz around the cabin like an age-slowed bee while I waited inside, not wanting to stand out in the field like some overseer, inspecting his work.

When he was done he'd pull up between the cabin door and fire pit, and I'd be there to greet and thank him. I didn't know what financial arrangement Bex's family had with Albert—whether the same mysterious source that had been keeping the electricity and telephone going all these years had also been keeping him—but I'd slip him a twenty every so often to ensure that everything stayed sound between us. He'd act shy and scrunch the bill into his pants, mumbling his thanks. Then we'd stand there looking at the freshly mowed field.

"Well . . . at least now you can come and go easier," he'd say.

"Oh, yeah. It's much better. Thank you."

"This way you can come and go."

"Yeah. No, it's great. Thanks."

"House is still standing!"

"Yeah. Still here."

The cabin lecture would usually follow. If I already had my evening fire going, we'd talk about my dinner.

"Eatin snake tonight?" he'd ask with a broad, toothless grin.

Albert is terrified of snakes. I'd told him about the ones in the fire pit, embellishing the story for his benefit with descriptions of my favorite snake recipes. He seemed particularly taken with the idea of baby snakes on a bed of the fresh fiddlehead ferns that I'd found growing this spring along the Wickerby entrance road. There wasn't a conversation between us afterward in which the subject of eating snake didn't come up.

"Yeah, Albert. Barbecued baby snake tonight," and he'd walk off to his tractor, wringing his hat and giggling.

It wasn't until the end of August that he finally entered

the cabin. I can't recall why exactly, something about the vertical support beams, perhaps, but I remember thinking it a mere pretext to work his way inside. He made a show of checking the alignment of the beams but was clearly more interested in sizing me up, my living arrangement.

Shy about coming too far in, he kept bobbing and weaving his way around the woodstove, staring all the while over my shoulder at the papers and open notebooks on the corner oak table, trying to steal as many looks as he could at the trappings of my work, sensing, I imagined, some rigor there, and I thought then of the Latin root for the word *verse:* "versus," meaning a turning of the plow.

About a week or so later, I was at the corner table, working into the early evening, the radio playing, when I felt a presence in the cabin and turned to see Albert's capped and crooked silhouette in the doorway.

"Writin a book?" he yelled.

"Yes," I said, getting up and starting toward him, shy myself now, "a book," not knowing what it was I was up to at that point exactly beyond a kind of extended note-taking, something to leave open on a table here for Bex, the story of my stay in her house, perhaps the last stay for anyone at Wickerby.

"It's a book about you, Albert," I said, steering him out the door, and he grabbed his cap from his head, and he started to laugh.

THE WASPS KEEP DRIFTING in through my windows, expending their brief lives in my warmth. The phone rings again. Lucy's ears lift slightly. I let the machine answer. More barking.

Downstairs, Desert Sax is really jamming now. People hurry past the Top of the World. Rooftop picnickers step across from building to building to the far end of Lincoln Place for a look down at the action. The man in the house of refuse hangs up his phone, walks to the end of Lincoln, turns right and then disappears into the fair crowd.

I watch everyone rushing along the avenue. They seem, like me now, to want to fly their own bodies, to perch somewhere outside and above the plodding disappointment of flesh and then ride with the pigeons this vessel of high-windowed rooms away, ride it further and faster away from that still, quiet hilltop where Wickerby teeters tonight, the saxophone reeling now across the Top of the World, notes fraying into building lights, lights staying notes on the air.

I'm writing it down now, Bex, in the Wickerby diary, how we are both places at once and never fully at home in either: all of us at once Wickerby and the urge to leave it; at once the woods and the disposition to desert them; all of us ongoing arguments with our flesh, exiles of our own inventions, and, always, inhabitants of a time that seems to move too fast.

Outside now, beneath the newly repaved parkway, beneath this whole bristling matrix of streets and dreaming spires; of arriving flights and the delicate tiptoe of changing traffic lights into the outer darkness, the earth just lies there. We keep stoking its furnaces with our bones, keep dressing up its darknesses with our cities, but as it neither hurries along nor waits for us, we pretend to go on without it, to be its exception, so far now into this world of our own making, so steeped in the whir and ping of our inventions that, like the pigeons across the way, we look for refuge and repose in the broken nooks and sills of our past creations, in the very look and feel of our own cast-off dies and moldings.

At one of the fair stalls I passed this morning, there's a display of old photographs and lithographs of Eastern Parkway. I purchased one that dates back to before the turn of the century. It shows the parkway soon after its completion. My building isn't there yet. In fact, none of the apartment buildings that now line my street have been constructed. There are just parallel rows of newly planted trees stretching through a wide-open plain, with a few scattered houses on the periphery of Crown Heights. Horse-drawn trolleys, hackneys and drays pass along the roadway's central median. Women in long bustled dresses with coats and parasols, men in suits with top hats and walking sticks, stroll down the promenade.

As I stare at the photo now, I feel that play of the past upon our minds, that illusion of a slower, more grounded day. But to the people in the photo, walking out on the promenade over a century ago—looking upon their surroundings with the same essential alignment of cells as you and I; with the same hearts buoying them from one breath to the next—it was simply a day, a Sunday, perhaps, like this one, and there was time enough for languor and yet not enough time, and, in the back of everyone's minds, was the same abiding fear of lost gradualness, the same illusion of a world speeding away on the back of our own unbridled industry.

"Things are in the saddle," Emerson proclaimed, "and they ride mankind." Mechanical looms, carding machines and spinning jennys were thrumming away in Brooklyn's textile mills. Cross-country railroads and steam-powered elevated trains were hastening eyes past cityscapes. Down the street, the Brooklyn Bridge had just gone up, the longest single suspension ever of steel through air, that day's equivalent of a moon launch, the architect, Washington Roebling, having to watch the completion of the flight from the bed of his top-floor, harbor-front apartment, too sick with the bends from all the dives he'd made into the riverbed caissons in order to ground such an unprecedented leap. Across from the Grand Army Plaza, where there had long been a barren stretch of rocky glacial moraine, Olmsted and Vaux were using giant earthmovers and new tree-moving machines to erect the very woods and glades we now seek as a stay against this day's clamor and speed. And straight south of Prospect Park, out by Bex's old house at Sea Gate, a great, fearful, play-city of modern inventions was rising against the skies of Coney Island, "Dreamland" and "Luna Park," their towers strung with thousands of Edison's new electric lights like a prefigurement of the Manhattan skyline, and the world's first roller coasters ran there and ferris wheels and motion pictures, and train rides to the North Pole, and rockets to the moon, and mechanical horses that raced "half a mile in half a minute," the sign out front scolding the fearful: DON'T BE A GLUMSTER. BE A STEEPLECHASER!

We've long resisted our own mechanisms, blamed them for our recurring sense of life's acceleration. Human beings make for such timorous, self-doubting creators, incapable of that objective remove that we often ascribe to our Creator, who set everything in motion and then turned his back upon it. We are forever confusing ourselves with the things we make, worrying that they will somehow overtake or desert us.

"We've moved to a whole new speed in how we live," the man who went to live with the Amish said. But it's not, of course, that we or our lives are going any faster. A day yawns as widely before us as it did a medieval monk and deserts us with equal dispatch. The dizzying distractions of our mechanisms notwithstanding, and, perhaps, to some degree because of them, we can all still recognize in our lives the plight of the prisoner who, at the start of his sentence, can't conceive of surviving the grinding slowness of his days but who, upon his release, can't believe those days have already passed him by.

Our lives are going no faster. The things we make are, and we can't accompany them, especially the computer, our minds' augment just as industrial machines are the body's. With the latter, at least, there are places to which our hands can report to help physically guide the material work. But it's the fleet aphysicality of the computer's work that so disorients us, leaves us in the lurch, makes our minds run wild with the notion that we are somehow inventing our own physical obsolescence.

This, I've come to understand after so many days of staring out into the deep blankness of a Wickerby hillside, ' after so many afternoon walks through the slow, long-lived silences of those woods, is our ongoing condition, to perpetually reinvent the trappings of our inherent unease over our own mortality, to be forever stranded by the fear of advancing age and the aura of our own inventions within what—because we remain the same—appears to be an evermore untenable present.

It's not unlike the feeling I have when I walk from this building to the Brooklyn harbor front, follow Eastern Parkway past the Grand Army Plaza, then head far down Union Street to the edge of the Gowanus Canal, an old, narrow ship channel dug back in the late 1840s from the Gowanus Bay in through the back streets of a residential, working-class neighborhood called Carroll Gardens, formerly the industrial northeast end of Red Hook.

The canal's thick wooden wharves were once lined with foundries, ink and paint factories, flour and paper mills, coal, lumber and brick yards, and a huge gasworks. Now only a few gravel and concrete yards remain, and, with the shift to container shipping and truck deliveries, the waterway itself is used only once a week by the same oil tanker, making its regular Wednesday-night delivery to a petroleum storage facility located at the canal's far north end.

The tanker is nearly as wide as the wharves and has to bump and squeak its way between them, leaving plenty of time for the bridge-tender on shore to drive from one control house to the next in order to flip the switches that lift, split and, at Carrol Street, retract along railroad tracks the canal's different back-street bridges. The tanker passes so slowly that you can stand on shore and see the crew members through the porthole windows, sitting in the ship's galley sipping coffee and playing cards, the tall, dark riggings on the ship deck above them inching past Manhattan's brightly lit office towers, almost touchable, in the background.

Standing there, it's as though you've got your feet firmly planted in the past and yet are looking beyond into a world of synaptic travel and thought. Somehow, we and the course of our days are more akin to the motion of that tanker, and yet our minds seem to be propelling us further into that sheer backdrop of lighted squares, where a mere twitch of speculative figures produces another idle millionaire, and the shapes of machines don't even begin to suggest the work they do.

Far out my window now, I can see the lighted peaks of the Brooklyn Bridge—"harp and altar, of the fury fused," as the poet Hart Crane described it some thirty years after its completion, when he was living in the very same apartment that Washington Roebling did, looking out each night at the bridge's "swift unfractioned idiom, immaculate sigh of stars."

But for us it seems the very symbol of a more gradual and weighty past. We can have no like embodiment today of the vast distances we've bridged, nothing that is, as the Brooklyn Bridge was back then, at once the actual and the imaginative leap, the deed and the monument to it; no one structure that both takes us and symbolically tells us where we are going.

I remember an afternoon years ago, walking into "Rocket Park," a stretch of lawn inside the entrance to the NASA Space Center in Houston, Texas. They have an Apollo rocket there tipped sideways and separated into its different stages, each stage set high up on metal stilts. It takes only a minute to go from base to tip, and yet somehow there's no way of taking it all in; no good way, it seems, of even describing it: "The engines in this stage," read one of the signs set on small pedestals before each section, "make the sound equivalent of 40,000 stereos playing hard rock at full volume."

Just ahead of me, a man was standing alone, hat in hand, looking up. He had on a plain gray business suit like the ones my father would wear to his tool-and-die plant office each day. I could see the man's eyes slowly roving, back and forth, over the length of the sectioned rocket—the now-"fractioned" idiom—as though he was unable to complete the thought, to encompass that divide between our unchanged physical selves and the disembodied, un-inhabitable places to which our machines now propel us.

He tried to explain this all to me once, I think, my father; to give me the rudiments of the long-unfolding re-creation myth by which we give our work over to machines and seem to leave ourselves behind in the process.

For years, I had no idea that he worked alongside machines, that he was a tool-and-die man. My only clue was the connection I happened to make one day between the strange smell he brought home on his suits each evening from the plant and the one that emanates from the back of a television. I still remember, as though it were part of some exotic wilderness trek, the first time I ventured behind the console TV set in our Flatlands' living room, peered in through the perforated back panel at the mini-cityscape of soldered circuitry and lighted cathode tubes, and took in that warm, high-pitched, acrid odor.

"Bakelite," my father called it, a plastic compound they used in the making and preserving of parts, a detail which contributed greatly to my abiding conception of the mechanical as something organic, alive, a conception that was to be permanently cast in my mind the day he first took me to see a tool-and-die machine.

We were off on one of our regular Sunday outings, this

one taking us beyond Brooklyn to visit the Statue of Liberty, but we just missed the last ferry, and I soon found myself being yanked along deserted city streets, the flailing pennant of an outsized adult rage. We were headed nowhere in particular, but then midway along some shadowed block in that ghostly air of stilled commerce that pervades lower Manhattan on a Sunday, plumes of street steam rising as though from the earth's own huge, idling engine, we stopped, and there was my father, lecturing to me excitedly before a dirt-caked shop window, its shallow inner ledge littered with random bits of piping, some screws, bolts and bearings, a window that you or I in a million city strolls would have strolled right past.

Cupping my hands against the glass, I peered into a room filled with massive gray, hulking shapes, used tool-and-die machines, my father told me, similar to those that he still had in his plant—lathes, grinders, planers, milling and drilling machines—with names like Hardinge, Cincinnati, Bridgeport embossed in silver letters across their sides, all of them standing there twenty deep in the shadows like guests at some soiree for steel.

Each one looked very different, and yet they all looked like nothing else but one another: like clumsily rendered men, the giant, anvil-armed men of a Thomas Hart Benton mural, hybrids of metal and urge, at once the worker and the wielded tool, rising up from an iron bed into a column or "knee," as my father called it, which supports the worktable above which loomed all the working armature—drills, feed rods, spindles, turrets, a "head box" full of controls and, protruding here and there, like truncated limbs, the knobs, levers and stops to which human hands report in order to guide each machine in manipulations of metal that our hands haven't the strength to make.

These machines, he was saying, are, in essence, us. They are our own best wishes for our hands: the representation, in a more precise and hardened form, of a primeval impulse to pick up a piece of raw material and make something from it. I can still see my father standing there, hands and mouth contorting, trying to speak for the machines themselves but unable to find words elemental enough, having to mime, in the end, the various motions by which each one, with its mounted, precision tool, shapes a piece of metal against a molded die, punching out the same part, one after the next: a screw, a clamp, a phono plug, an alligator clip, a nut, a bolt—all the anonymous disengaged parts of this object world that ticks, thrums and whorls its way around me here tonight.

The ancestry of any object I could think of, he said, minute or massive, could invariably be traced back to a tool-and-die machine—from the hinges on a pair of eyeglasses, to the little tool kit you buy to fix those hinges, to the parts for the machines that formed the frame and lenses of those glasses, or the lenses, for example, of the periscope through which a naval officer wearing those glasses might peer, to the huge iron hull sections of the submarine from which that periscope rises.

The very sidewalk we were standing on that day and the tools used to build it were shaped by tool and die, as was the stone, steel and glass of the buildings around us and the equipment used to erect them, and the light posts, and street signs and all the cars. It was as though I was being shown a whole other substrata of reality, as if beneath that rising street steam there was some Jules Vernian, middle-world civilization of man-machines whose sole, sacrificial function it is to manufacture and maintain the unquestioned surface sheen of our days. Indeed, the very machines we were looking at were all made of parts fashioned by tool-and-die machines, and they, in turn, made the parts for the newer tool-and-die models that were already replacing the ones there before us in that window.

It was, in effect, the story of mechanical evolution that he was telling me, and while that's not an easy tale to animate, for my father it had the kind of satisfyingly definitive origins and linkages that our own evolutionary history sorely lacks. On his shelves he had books like *Studies in the History of Machine Tools* and *A Short History of Technology*—which, at nearly a thousand pages, makes one shudder to contemplate the long version. I have all of them with me now, books that detail from the very beginning of civilization the attempt to reproduce ourselves mechanically, starting with the simplest movements of our hands.

On the wall above me, there's a framed print from one of the books, a bas relief from an Egyptian tomb dating back to the second century B.C.: two men kneeling before one of the first handmade lathes, its crude turrets and spindles turning a piece of wood in place as a mounted cutting tool is brought to bear upon it.

A variety of tool-and-die mechanisms were invented over the centuries, but the parts they produced would vary in shape and size just as the bowls from a potter's wheel do. It would take civilization more than two millennia to achieve what my father would call low "tolerances"—a term I've always thought curious because it means the exact opposite of what it suggests: a strict intolerance for any variation in the size and shape of a manufactured part, from one part to the next.

Most American children hear about the deeds of Washington, Jefferson and Lincoln. For me it was tales of the seventeenth-century European clock makers who, in answer to the demand for more accurate timepieces, finally built the first precision tool-and-die machines capable of turning out exactly calibrated, replicable parts, an achievement that would initiate the endless cycle of machines begetting the standardized, readily assembled parts for other machines and, in effect, change the shape of history.

"We can blame it all on the gentle clock maker," my father would say with a wry smile. There was little hand-wringing in our house about the possible dehumanizing effects of our expanding industry, a very low tolerance for the classic Romantic protestations about machines driving the artisans from their workshops, severing workers from the finished product, and thus reducing them to mere fragments of the whole.

To my father, our technology is precisely what enables us to be more human. The most advanced ancient cultures, he was fond of pointing out, were those that delegated their physical labor to slaves. We give machines our immediate burdens—whether it's the crunching of metal or, with computers, of numbers—in order to free ourselves, as the inhabitants of the first large agrarian settlements did, to pursue new creations, even if workers get displaced in the process. "Workers," my father would say, "have to be retooled just as machines do."

I thought of that statement one afternoon a few years ago when I found myself walking through an international manufacturing and technology exhibition in Chicago. The "Factory of the Future," as the exhibition was described in one of the promotional catalogs, was actually closed to the general public, and when I was stopped at the front entrance and asked to declare my official affiliation on a registration form, I somehow managed to dredge up the name of my father's long-defunct company. I had, after all, gone to that exhibition as his emissary, had gone to satisfy a curiosity about, almost a yearning for, machinery that he long ago instilled in me. Within moments I was handed a plasticized ID tag, still warm, bearing my name, the same as my father's, and, in bold black letters: National Tech-Tronics. I pinned the tag to my lapel and walked ahead into the convention center.

In the factory of the future, it would come as no surprise, the machines look nothing like the ones my father had shown me that Sunday in lower Manhattan, though I did find an assortment of those behind a set of what looked like white hospital-room curtain dividers with computer printout signs taped to them that read "Tool and Die Museum"—a few lathes and planers looking now like hunched-over, arthritic seamstresses, unable to thread their own needles. Still, the new machines, just like those old models, all resembled one another, all had that sheer, mono-lithic form of modern buildings and computers. There was no visible armature: no knees, no places for the hands of a worker like my father to report, no suggestion anymore either of us, their maker, or of what they've been made to do. Just huge, rectangular, glass-enclosed units with an outer keyboard control panel and a big window that looks onto the high-speed, water-cooled work being done within.

Exhibit after exhibit, it was the same: machines working at a fever pitch while a man in a pastel-colored smock stood idly by monitoring the muted whine and click of parts being shaped and then deposited in bins. I saw three-dimensional, five-axis, laser machines, omniturn machines, vertical and horizontal multi-turret machining centers with bidirectional tool selection and rapid traverse rates. I saw machines with wide-range gripping force, and dead-length positioning.

At the center of the exhibition, I came upon a display of two robot arc welders. Their welding tips looked like little swan heads that would rise up periodically from their work, come face-to-face as though to exchange a few words, and then swivel back down. At one point a factory welder, wearing his union hat, approached. He watched as one steaming, newly welded part after the next got dropped into a bin. Before walking away, he stepped up and, with a pair of tongs, lifted one of the parts for inspection.

"Pretty damn good," he said.

Downstairs, the music stops. J is talking into the microphone, making another speech about the great potential of our neighborhood, thanking all of those who contributed to the First Annual Washington Avenue Extravaganza. People drift, aimlessly, past the remaining fair booths. Children are lining up for their last rides on the Top of the World. I can hear the tugboats now from New York Harbor, their mournful whistles nudging along this slow, timeless vessel of a night.

At times I wish my father had not steered me past that window of tool and die, had not so tellingly animated for me the inanimate. I hardly make a distinction between the two anymore. To me, we and machines are, despite our divergent authorship, essentially the same, are both uniquely ordered, ephemeral arrangements of atoms, brief stays against the universe's prevailing disorder. I can't see a machine now without seeing something of ourselves. Can't cross a bridge without thinking of the different bolts that bind it: the ceaseless, shifting weight upon them, the winter's bite, the summer's swell in every joint. I can't see this room or its furnishings; can't see the whole lighted array of rooms around me or the one that fell like a star and broke open on the sidewalk around the man in the house of refuse; I can't see the streets that bind these buildings, or the parked cars, or the bent metal trash container on the corner of Washington and Lincoln, or even our trash— the plastic bags snagged in the upper tree branches, and the tangled gleams of unraveled cassette tape in the newly refilled parkway's promenade grass—as anything but what they all are: extensions of us, and therefore, of nature; pieces of the earth taken up and pressed against our variously shaped dies to form the parts that suit our briefly passing purposes.

Still, if there is a tradeoff for having had the weight of the world's objects added to the peculiar burden of being one of its conscious inhabitants, it's that I don't fear our machines the way so many of us still do, don't think they are lording over our lives, or making them move too fast. I don't, in the end, blame machines for our inherent discomfort over the passage of time, a discomfort rooted in the simple fact that we are the only ones who mark time's passing.

Often now, I find myself marking the nearly twenty years since my father's death by the inventions he's missed. I have this ridiculous dream in which he makes a sudden reappearance to me, and I waste all of our brief time together showing him the things that I know he hasn't seen—the VCR, the cellular phone, the CD player, the latest laptop computer. I can't explain how anything works.

Sometimes we even end up walking together through that technology show. I escort him past the different exhibits, past all the new, muted machines which perhaps, in their very limblessness, are eerie harbingers of some future us: all head box, the rest having withered away from disuse. He never spoke to me about how the story ends, any more than someone millions of years ago could have said of the first shoreward-flopping amphibians that their scales would one day turn to feathers and their forelimbs, with time and will, to wings.

At the back of the convention center, we arrive at the exhibit about technology of the distant future: high-speed, parallel-processing computers built around processing vats of our own DNA; human-machine interface, man-robot hybrids; rooms made of virtual walls, the design and makeup of which can be changed with the flip of a switch; micro-machines that fit upon the head of a pin; and nano-machines, too small to see, the end of work as we know it: millions of retooled, thoroughly compliant molecules, willed air, assembling and reassembling for whatever purpose suits our shifting needs.

In the dream, we review the future in silence and then walk back out through the convention center, through that endless airy room of idle men tending their own displacement, the very story to which he first introduced me, the one that, even as we continue to shape the dies of its distant outcome, we can still only ever inhabit or abide momently. There's a natural disjuncture between mechanical and biological evolution.

This, I suppose, is the part of the story that I could tell him now, how—for all the fuss about our machines and for all of their apparent affect upon our lives—oddly incidental they remain to us, to the same old flesh-and-bone bulks of you and me, going along within this day, within this longing.

I remember one night this summer at Wickerby, sitting up late, watching the little portable TV. My one working channel happened to be showing the classic, 1930s Hollywood version of Victor Hugo's *The Hunchback of Notre Dame*. As the film opens, a priest is being shown the newly invented printing press. He looks away at one point and stares out across a courtyard at the Notre Dame cathedral with all its symbolic statuary and stories in stained glass. Cathedrals, he says, were the handwriting of the past but with the printing press, the burden of storytelling had now shifted to the printed page.

And the thought occurred to me that it was this shift of burden that has, over time, resulted in the pared-down, monolithic statements of modern architecture, in the same way that printers, word processors, copy machines and a variety of other recording devices have all obviated the need for poetry to rhyme, rhyme originally serving as a memory device that would help a listener to musically lock a thought or image in their mind. As a result, we now have the mostly rhymeless, free verse of modern poetry. Sheer buildings, rhymeless poems, and limbless machines: the shape of our creations and the imperative behind them may change, but not us or the impulse to create.

I could tell my father now the part about how we'll continue to exaggerate the effects of our own inventions as a natural protective mechanism against them, a way of gradually embracing their apparent otherness. Time, which is often said to heal the pain of a loss, also deadens the so-called shock of the new. Somehow the "Brave New World" has a way of becoming the bland old everyday.

I could tell him the part about how we'll be able to go on giving machines all of our burdens, all except for one, an argument with their own flesh, a fear of their own mortality, that one catch, squiggle, snag of consciousness that inspires all we invent and yet still leaves us stranded out here alone on the far, shiny-surfaced side of our inventions, listening, waiting for our own completion.

Tonight, when the fair is long over, and the street noise has settled down, and the whole city emits that faint, high-

pitched whir of an idle office machine, I'll lie back in bed
and, near sleep, hear again, that man in the single-engine
plane fly over, his lone engine droning at the far edges of
the sky. I used to think of him as speed itself, the instant
bearer of night, the one who, like God, sees so far and yet
sees no one. But now, he's become to me the very sound
and weight of the past, like a horse-drawn wagon down a
narrow cobblestone street, modernity's milk cart.

ALBERT DID COME UP to the cabin one day merely to lend me a hand. He must have heard across the valley the muffled scrapes of my plunged shovel blade because there he suddenly was, making his way up the entrance road with his tractor and backhoe. He pulled up alongside the rectangular section of field I'd staked off just beyond the butternut tree, and with two or three quick passes of the backhoe, rendered my physically-disaffected-modern-man's afternoon of restorative digging into a split-second garden plot.

He hopped down and mumbled something about how that at least ought to get me started. This is as close as Albert ever comes to an outward display of affection, and I knew to scale back any gratitude I might express so as not to embarrass him. I said it sure would, and then the two of us stood there a moment in silence, regarding the sweet-smelling, upturned rows. Albert told me all about the potatoes he grew each year near his woodpile, and then he just waved a hand and left.

In the course of loosening and sifting through my garden's soil, I kept finding pieces of old farm implements—harness rigging, horseshoes, the counterbalance of an old steelyard—all heavily cankered with rust and corrosion. It was as if the entire workings of a long-ago Wickerby farm day had suddenly seized up in a rainstorm and then collapsed in place into the earth. Someone in Bex's family had begun saving these artifacts years ago. They nearly cover the cabin's back wall. I put my pieces aside and later added them to the collection.

I made four posts out of sections of an old pasture fence that I found inside the A-frame toolshed. After digging holes in each corner of the plot, I sank the posts and then strung them with some heavy chicken wire that I'd purchased at the hardware store in Fitch Bay. I even made myself a working gate with hinges and a hook-and-eye latch on it to let myself in and out.

As for what to plant, my choices were somewhat arbitrary. The guy working the hardware store counter advised me to go with zucchini, beets, carrots and green beans. I tossed in a packet of bibb lettuce seeds for good measure, a decision I'd end up patting myself on the back for, as sweet, luminous green bibb heads were soon sprouting from their bed—my first garden's surprise bumper crop.

Still, looking back on it now, the things I grew seem to me secondary to the experience of planting them. I'm thinking specifically of that moment when I opened the individual seed packets and first saw the tiny, wizened specks that were billed to become my beets, beans, carrots, bibbs and squash. It required a prodigious leap of faith to drop one or two of those near-microscopic motes into the shallow indents of dirt that I'd made for them upon the back of this planet's cold, rolling immensity, and then to cover them over, leave them and expect something to come from that.

What I remember best about my garden, however, is the simple, sense-leveling effect of toiling in it. In the months that followed, whenever I got down on my hands and knees there to work, I would think of a man I met one night years ago in a pub in Cornwall, England. He introduced himself as Fred Kurnow The Earth Stopper. He just plopped down into the booth where I was sitting, and pointed up at one of the hundreds of pictures on the wall above my table. It was a photo of a fox hunt, the traditional shot of the participants after the fact, sitting up on their horses in full regalia in front of the lodge, shotguns held in the crook of the arm, the barrels pointed either straight up or down to the side. At the far left of the frame, out in front of the assembled hunting dogs, was a decidedly rumpled figure in a big leather coat up on his horse, a fox hound in the saddle beside him, and a short spade dangling from the side-saddle pouch.

"Urth stopurrrh!" he kept repeating in his thick Cornish accent, which sounds like English run through a hay baler. After a few more beers, however, I'd achieved just the right measure of mental sluggishness to make Cornish sound clear, and learned that an earth stopper is, in effect, the prime mover of the hunt, the one who rides out in the wee hours of the morning before the first horn and stops up all the holes where a fox might hide, thus prolonging the chase.

Once the hunt started, Fred Kurnow was already asleep, either out in the fields somewhere beside his horse and dog or in the hayloft of the barn behind the hunting lodge. By evening, he'd be there at the pub. For over sixty years that had been his life, nights in the pub letting go of the world, days of stopping it up with his hands. I have no idea what he did on the days when there was no hunt, whether one makes a good enough living from earth stopping to have it be their sole source of income, but then, Fred Kurnow was someone who didn't seem to require much. He had no family, no land, just his dog and horse, and an endless supply of holes to stop.

Aside from the bibb lettuce, my garden at Wickerby yielded me a solid, steady output of green beans, a crop of somewhat stunted, shrively beets and carrots, and—all the past diary entries about yearly bountiful harvests of zucchini notwithstanding—not one zucchini.

I was able to reap these modest rewards right up to my departure yesterday, even picking some beans and bibbs to bring back with me. The rest I left to the foragers and the coming frost. I think of them up there still on the vine, withering in the cold, think of them and of my father, of me and Bex, and of this whole clustered trillium of lights, all turning with the earth tonight inexorably homeward.

·THE·
WAY BACK

FROM NEARLY MID-JUNE until late August, I'd see my wood-chuck friend less and less. Sometimes in the early morning, I'd find him in the foundation nook beneath the front window. Occasionally, I'd catch a glimpse of him across the cabin's north field, moving along the perimeter of the small patch of woods that begins on the far side of the old apple tree and runs two hundred yards or more to the base of the low stone wall and barbed pasture fence that borders the far edges of Byron Eliott's place.

But just when I'd concluded that the little whistle pig—as the Indians are said to have called them—had finally grown bored with me and my doings at Wickerby, Lucy showed up one August evening out by the fire pit with the woodchuck in her jaws.

I had, in the by-then-distant wake of the Rasteedy

affair, actually come to admire Lucy's various gestures, however half-baked, in the general direction of retrieving her primal instincts: her hopeless darts into the wooded distance after a deer, or her utter conviction (despite the Dalmation's official designation as a non–sporting breed) that she was a champion bird dog. She'd assume the point position in the middle of our walks through Blackberry Field, and I'd never take her seriously until the afternoon I decided to venture out into the spellbound region of her fixed stare, and triggered there a heart-stopping explosion of grouse from the tall field grass.

I was aware of her that evening out by the fire, heard her frantically foraging under the hem of the lilac bush as I sat back, sipping bourbon, trying to guess what creature was fortunate enough to have Lucy as its pursuer. Then all the rustling stopped, and I turned to see a wide-eyed, deeply shocked Dalmatian, standing at attention before me with the woodchuck stuck there limply, awkwardly, in her mouth. He kept looking back up at Lucy with what seemed to be profound impatience, as though he just wanted her to get on with it.

The whole picture looked wrong. It reminded me of the time I went fishing as a kid one summer vacation and, not wanting to return empty-handed, picked up a dead cat-fish that I'd found on shore, slipped my hook through its underbelly, and bore it proudly home to show my decid-edly unimpressed father.

Lucy is not in the habit of minding me. It may have been the fervor of my shout, reliving as I was at that moment the horror of Rasteedy's murder, but when I told her to "Drop it!" she did so instantly, and we both watched her prey waddle back off under the lilac bush.

The entire episode, odd though it was, struck me as being wholly consistent with everything else I'd experienced with this woodchuck thus far. But when the same scenario unfolded twice more in the following week, it finally dawned on me, after all those months of wild conjecturing about the animal's unique makeup and possible motives, that what I had on my hands was one very old, tired and, most likely, sick woodchuck. One who was trying to die but taking a ridiculously long time to do it. In fact, I began to get the distinct feeling that the creature was looking for a bit of a shove, and when Lucy got ahold of him yet again one evening just a couple of weeks ago out past the old apple tree, I decided to oblige.

It is, of course, only because of that catch, that snag in our DNA, that we humans get into a situation like this one in which we have to decide to put an animal out of what we deem to be its misery when, in fact, the creature may be quite content with the manner of its passing.

In truth, the whole business seemed to me a horrible cliché, something I'd seen countless times before in Disney nature movies, and yet there was a feeling of complete naturalness and inevitability about it, as though all my thoughts and actions were predicated on some a priori knowledge about how to behave in such instances. Go into the cabin, I said to myself, get the gun, shoot the animal in the head and then bury him in the woods.

Of course, there was no gun at Wickerby. All I could find in the cabin's junk corner by the fuse box was an old unstrung fiberglass bow. There were, too, those random golf clubs, but I wasn't about to go at my woodchuck with a two-iron.

I knew he was out there, waiting for me in that patch of woods beyond the apple tree. I'd followed him there after the previous encounter with Lucy. He retreated into a small burrow at the base of an old poplar. A moment later, he reemerged, positioning himself at the edge of the hole, allowing me to take a good, long look at him; sprigs of white-gray fur rimming his snout and forelimbs.

I would eventually choose as my instrument of mercy one of the loosened boulders from the framework of the fire pit, and was heading toward the woods with it when the thought occurred to me that Albert might very well have a gun around his place. Bex had told me once about Albert, years back, posing himself as an avid hunter to Bex's aunt because he'd heard her say that she'd rather buy a hunter his meat than let him shoot animals. Albert ate pretty well in those years.

This did not necessarily mean that he actually owned a gun, but I felt certain that anyone who's lived in the country as long as Albert has must have a firearm somewhere on the premises, or, at the very least, know someone in the area who does.

I locked Lucy in the cabin and started down the Wickerby entrance road. Smoke was spewing from Albert's chimney. He was usually back from his day's chores by dusk, and though we were just a few weeks into September, the days were already noticeably shorter. I crossed over the main road, walked up Albert's dirt drive, went around back and knocked on his door, both halves closed this time, his cats gathering at my feet.

It took him a long time to answer.

"House fall down yet?"

I explained to him the situation and all the usual insistent play went out of Albert. Now he, too, seemed locked into that a priori mode. He bowed his head, shuffled his feet and went away into the recesses of his one-room existence, returning a moment later with a big red coat cradled sideways in his arms, the coat's empty sleeves wrapped tightly.

We walked over to his parked tractor, Albert saying over and over now, "Don't like to do the thing!" He got up in the tractor seat, set the red coat in his lap, and started the engine. I hopped on behind him, my feet perched on the tractor's narrow side runner plates, my hands on Albert's shoulders. It was the first and the only time I touched him. We rode together in silence down his drive and then up Wickerby's long wooded hillside, through the tunnel of already-turning leaves.

At the top of the road, I directed Albert to the right, past the cabin and the fire pit, past the lilac-rimmed maple and the apple tree. He pulled to the edge of the north woods, shut the engine off, got down with his red coat and began to unravel it. "Don't like to do the thing!" he said.

The coat fell to the grass. Albert held in his hands what appeared to me to be the first rifle ever built. It looked like the wooden prototype for a gun, or like the mock guns given to drill teams for marching. An old .22 caliber rifle, it was just a metal bore resting in a burnished, oily wood stock, with a little ball-headed steel bolt on the side for opening and closing the ammo chamber. He took from his shirt pocket a small wooden box and slid open the lid to reveal one last row of ammo, the gold shells set into their bullet-shaped felt inlays, like fine pieces of jewelry.

He loaded. We walked together into the woods. The woodchuck was waiting there just as I'd left him. Albert didn't hesitate. He put the tip of the gun barrel right on the animal's head. I watched him turn away, and then squeeze his eyes closed just as his finger did the trigger. There was a muffled pop.

I looked back down to see the woodchuck, still waiting there, staring up at me as he had been all spring and summer, with that vaguely bored, bemused expression on his face. Albert had already started away, mumbling to himself about not liking to do the thing. Either he'd aimed at the very hardest spot in a woodchuck's skull or his gun was as pathetic as it appeared. I probably could have thrown a bullet harder than his rifle could shoot one.

I called him back. He seemed very upset now. In one quick, determined motion, he reloaded, put the barrel tip back on the animal's head and pulled the trigger, the woodchuck's entire body lifting this time, then settling, bonelessly, down, eyes shut tight.

Albert was already at the edge of the woods when I looked up. I went to see him to his tractor. He picked up his coat from the grass and wrapped it around the gun. I told him thanks. Then I said that I'd buy him more bullets.

I'd seen that he was nearly out and wasn't sure how easily he could get ahold of such things.

He mumbled an "Okay," gave a quick wave of his hand and got up on the tractor. Before starting the engine, he looked at me and said, with a bitter edge now, as though he felt I hadn't understood him before: "Noooo, bud aye mean, I don't like to do the thing!" Then he drove off down the hillside. I walked back over to the north woods, pushed the woodchuck's carcass fully into its burrow and then covered everything up with stones and dirt. One more Wickerby burial.

It was dark by then, and rather than standing over the fire pit, cooking with a flashlight, I decided to go inside the cabin and heat myself a can of soup for dinner. Afterward, Lucy and I sat up late by the woodstove. It was the first time I'd needed to light it since the spring, and by the time I went up to bed that night, the cabin was quite cozy. Still, I slept restlessly and, by first light, was wide awake to watch the bats come in.

Early on in the course of my stay at Wickerby I must have trained myself to wake up for this ritual because I rarely missed it. The first two or three bats would be my alarm. I'd never see them. They nested on the other side of the insulation lining the windowless south gable just above my bed. Immediately upon arriving, they'd exchange these quick, urgent volleys of bat-squeak. They may have been reporting to one another about the night's activities or calling in the rest of the troops, or both, but that ruckus was my cue to turn on my pillow and look across the loft toward the north gable's wide windows.

There, against the dawn sky, I'd watch the emerging outline of the plum tree's upper boughs and then the bats returning to them, hundreds of black, inward-folding flecks like felled autumn leaves returning in reverse time-lapse photography back up to their branches. It was as if the whole world was going in reverse, from summer into spring, the leaves closing into buds again and the buds into days of dormancy.

Once all the bats had returned, the squeaking in the south gable would stop, and I'd go back to sleep for another couple of hours. But a few days after I'd buried the woodchuck, the bats stopped coming altogether. It was mid-September. They were already on their way to a longer, winter's sleep, and I was beginning to think about leaving Wickerby.

Albert, I noticed, had been keeping to himself since the night of the woodchuck. He didn't visit once in the following week, and I actually found myself missing him.

Many times in the course of his lectures on the perils of inhabiting collapsing log cabins, he had detailed for me what he thought would be required to revive Wickerby. The first thing, he said, would be to get ahold of big ten-ton jacks and lift the cabin, one side at a time, off its original rock foundation in order to realign and bolster it with new rocks and cement. Otherwise, as Albert put it, "I'd be wastin time and money and wood for nuthin! Am I righ?"

He said that even with a new foundation, new cribbing would be necessary for extra support underneath the cabin floor along the main joists. New spruce logs—to be had at a bargain rate from Albert, of course—were also needed to replace the badly rotted ones, most of them in that southeast corner and along the base of the cabin's front side, but the remainder of the logs, he conceded, were in remarkably good condition for over a century and a half of wear.

Once all that was taken care of, he told me, I could tend to the more finicky jobs like fumigating the place, patching the roof, replacing the plumbing, the woodstove piping and broken windowpanes, and then mortaring the joints and window frames. The whole job Albert figured would run me about ten thousand dollars, rather cheap, I told him, although still about ten thousand more than I had.

There was, too, that other option of taking some stopgap measures that might actually allow Lucy and me to tough it out at Wickerby for a winter. With a few sheets of plywood, I figured I could board up from the inside—although at the probable expense of that ant citadel—the collapsing southeast corner, and at least keep out the driving snows and winds. I'd then reseal the broken windows with new sheets of heavy plastic; stock the cabin with lots of canned goods, dried soups and bourbon; park the car down at the base of the Wickerby entrance road for when the real snows came; arrest from their second life as nostalgia pieces the pair of old snowshoes hanging on the wall above the corner oak table; pile up maybe six or seven cords of split logs; and then hunker down in earnest, venture ever further into my terra incognita of isolation the already broad boundaries of which my far-flung near-wife was—with each new day of her wandering—steadily expanding.

I'd stay up there at Wickerby and make Bex come home to me, to the story of my travels, my insular wandering within her abandoned past. I'd go so far into myself that neither she nor I would recognize me. I'd entertain all of my thoughts and then go further, into thoughtlessness, and accompany that, and that of all the cabin's creatures, down to the most tiny and unseen. I'd compose librettos for every bug; become fluent, through a kind of will-less, osmotic listening, in all the mute dialects and hermetic hieroglyphs of the minute and the microscopic: bacteria, viruses, DNA, atoms—all the invisible matter that both informs and will soon inherit you and me, and this day and Wickerby's. I'd listen, over time, to the very matter of listening, and thereby learn how to wholly entertain—that is to say, without going to pieces—the mindless minutiae of our own makeup.

I'd go so far into solitude that some nights I'd even venture some of the bars near Wickerby, local watering holes over in the Vermont towns of Bee Bee or Derby Line, places which just getting to meant risking another encounter with the deranged U.S. border guard who detained me for no good cause one recent evening at the customs house in Bee Bee.

I often drove into the States over the summer to buy groceries and bourbon. Booze is heavily taxed in Canada to help pay for the country's universal health-care system, and while I vigorously support that arrangement in principle, I had, as a relatively impoverished American, little interest in doing so in practice. It so happens, however, that a good number of Canadians feel the same way, which is why Canadian customs officials charge a high tariff on any U.S. goods being brought back into their country, especially liquor.

To skirt this little obstacle, I devised a simple system, inspired in its way, of smuggling my bourbon back to Wickerby. I'd drive to the local Grand Union in Newport, Vermont, buy a gallon of water and a large jug of apple or prune juice, anything with brown-tinted glass. In the back corner of the Grand Union parking lot, I'd pour out the juice, wash the jar with the water and refill it with bourbon. It was always during these convoluted exchanges that I'd think of a remark that the painter Willem de Kooning once made regarding poverty: "The worst thing about it," he said, "is that it takes up so much of your time."

Now, the front end of these high-stakes smuggling missions was usually no bother. I didn't have the bourbon yet. The U.S. border guard would ask the usual perfunctory questions about where I lived in the States, where I was presently headed, and I was off. In fact, before long the guard would recognize my car and just wave me through. Guards do change posts, however, to keep them awake, I suppose, and this one evening that I'm referring to I got a particularly keen public servant.

"Where you from?"

"Brooklyn, New York." I always took great pleasure saying that in Bee Bee, Vermont.

"What's the purpose of your stay in Canada?"

"I'm staying at a place back up the road."

"Renting?"

"It belongs to my wife," I told him, not wanting to bother with the near-wife business.

"And what do you do?"

Here, I felt, we might be moving into uncharted waters, but then, he started it. "I'm a writer," I said, the rising inflection making it sound more like a question.

"Hmm," he answered. "What do you think of Garrison Keillor?"

Caught now completely off guard, I opted for the truth and said that I'd never read him. He eyed me very suspiciously. I could almost read his thoughts: "And you call yourself a writer? What are you trying to pull?" I felt my body tensing. This, I thought, will make for an interesting entry in the U.S. Customs arrest ledgers: suspect searched and seized in Bee Bee, Vermont, for not having read *The Prairie Home Companion*.

"I've read all his books," he announced. "In fact, I correspond with him."

"Really," I said, somewhat relieved by the shift of focus.

"Well, he hasn't written me back yet. Probably because I'm so mad at him."

I nodded.

"You're a writer," he began heatedly. "Maybe you can tell me why someone as talented and respected and popular as that man is, has to go and write a book filled with such filth and smut. . . ."

I still have no idea what book he was referring to, and while I found it difficult to conceive of anything even remotely ribald emanating from the pen of Garrison Keillor, I just sat there behind the wheel, nodding and shaking my head.

"Just to sell more books? Is this what we've come to? Anything for the almighty dollar?"

He carried on for a good ten minutes: the rampant proliferation of pornography, the loss of family values, the moral decline of an entire nation, all spearheaded by Garrison Keillor. In my rearview mirror, meanwhile, was a line of headlights backed up far into Canada. I made an obvious show of shifting into first gear and then revved the engine.

"What'd you say your name was again?" He took out a piece of paper and made me spell it out for him.

"Okay," he said. "I'll be keeping an eye out for you."

Of course, had I decided to stay at Wickerby, there were other crossing points not too far out of the way that I knew I could use, all for the pleasure of revisiting the Angus Ale House or the Passport Lounge, places where everyone at the bar turns in unison when a stranger enters, regarding him with the same suspicious, dead-eyed expression that I was beginning to note in my own countenance near the end of my stay at the cabin.

The fact is, I was becoming a bit too fond, even possessive of my loneliness. I was beginning to feel that contraction of the spirit I spoke of earlier; a general guardedness that I found particularly disagreeable because there seemed to be so little of interest left of me to guard.

It was not unlike the feeling I had years ago while attending "poetry-writing school." I began in earnest, seizing the opportunity to put down on paper and refine whatever it is I thought I had to say at the age of twenty-five. But before long I was just passing time there, cut off from the experiences and antagonisms, the urgencies and ideas that all conspire to make poetry, to make, as Robert Frost once defined a poem, "a figure of the will braving alien entanglements." I was left with nothing but a constant pre-occupation with the idea of being a poet, the empty asser-tion of the premise, the polishing of the pose.

In the end, the prospect of extending my stay at Wickerby became to me as untenable as the prolonged presence of the very hole in my street that first precipitated my departure. All of us here were drawn to that hole at first, the interruption of this day, the reminder of another day unfolding elsewhere. There's something deeply edify-ing about the destruction of a prominent edifice. Still, after a point, you need your street back, the traffic, the anony-mous to and fro, the passing dismissal of one another that paradoxically binds and buoys city dwellers.

I wanted to be back in the fray, to rejoin the so-called human argument, even this collapsed and compromised version of it; this troubled spot where, at least, when the ugliness does occur, we never have to hear "It's not the sort of thing that happens here!" invariably uttered on the nightly news by those who've just been disabused of the notion that theirs or any human dwelling place is immune to sordidness.

I wanted—like those crazed moths and countless other nameless flying things that embroidered the air around my book each night up in the cabin loft—the lights.

"What," I remember asking Bex as we sat up reading one night in bed at Wickerby, "did moths do before there were lights?"

"Not much," she said.

CLOSING UP A RUIN proved to be as absurd as trying to clean one, and far more sad. Still, I tried to leave things in such a way as to prompt Bex and me to return, small enticements, minor, tendable wounds: my garden, for one, neglected now and yet, indisputably, begun; or Rasteedy's cage, hanging beneath the butternut tree, wired open to the coming winter and its hearty holdouts—the sparrows and nuthatches, the tufted titmice and black-capped chickadees. Their food trays will need refilling long before spring.

And then there's Wickerby itself. I left it as I found it—in the balance—but left little indications there, as well, of a possible return. I put the spices and condiments up in the hanging baskets away from the mice, put the woodstove matches in a closed tin, and the little TV back in the upstairs wood chest where I'd found it. From beneath one of the brass beds in the loft, I took the plywood mattress board, brought it downstairs, sawed it into two pieces and nailed them over what seemed to me the cabin's most penetrable and inviting window—the front right one under which the woodchuck used to camp. Then, like the man downstairs in the house of refuse, I gave the place a good sweeping.

Yesterday morning, I got up early and made my bed. Albert, who had not been up to the cabin since he shot the woodchuck, must have heard me preparing to leave, and came up the hill on his tractor to give his cabin spiel one last time. After he left, I drained the pipes and turned off the power, even remembering to leave on that ridiculous pest-control device—one frail, flickering rampart against the onslaught that I knew would resume by the time I got halfway down the entrance road.

I swept the cabin some more, occasionally announcing, to no one in particular, both upstairs and down, my intention to return. The carpenter ants I told specifically. Then I took up my bags and backed out of the cabin, taking hold of the combination lock on the door latch and clicking it closed.

In addition to the diaries and the photo album and one large bag containing the last, viable vegetables that I could gather from my garden, I had in my possession some unexpected items from Bex's past: a pair of her old rubber Billy Boots, a wool sweater and an inexplicably beautiful rhomboidish ashtray with a deep, cloud-streaked blue sky painted across the dish, and the tiny letters "b" "e" "x" scratched into the lower-right corner.

All these items I actually had to buy back from Albert just a few days earlier at his yard sale. I had gone down to his house to give him the box of .22 bullets that I'd purchased for him at a sporting goods store during my final bourbon run to the States. I was a lot more nervous than usual going through Canadian customs that day, thinking that the combination of bourbon and live ammo would surely be enough to get me thrown in jail, and wouldn't that be something for Bex to come home to.

Bullets in hand, I walked down to the base of the Wickerby road and immediately noticed the chicken-scrawl YARD SALE sign that Albert had stuck beside his mailbox. A bit further up his dirt drive, all manner of junk was strewn in the grass, some of it propped up against the side of his house. Albert must have been watching, as usual, out the front window, because he suddenly appeared from the back of the house and walked down his drive as though trying to intercept me. I handed him the bullets. He barely looked at them, mumbled thanks.

"So, ya headin back, then?" he suddenly shouted, doing a more subdued bob and weave, pulling his cap off, rubbing his head with it.

I hadn't said a thing to him yet about my intentions, but these, too, he seemed to sense from across the valley.

"Yeah," I said, "going back to the city."

I glanced over at some of the goods he had set out— pairs of old boots, some empty picture frames, a washboard, an assortment of rusted tools, an old lawn mower.

A yard sale seemed to me an entirely un-Albert-like activity, and not a very lucrative one either, at least not that late in the season. By mid-September all the summer vacationers around nearby Georgeville have gone back to Montreal, and no more than fifteen, maybe twenty cars a day pass up and down the road between Albert's place and Wickerby. I wondered if he had hit on particularly hard times or if he was perhaps trying to raise money for a new tractor.

"So, Albert," I said, breaking the silence, "trying to get rid of some things."

"Ain't nuthin. Jus some junk," he muttered, shuffling in my direction now.

I thought it polite to express an interest, and that's when I happened to focus on one of the small, framed prints Albert had lying there in the grass. It was an old lithograph of "The Lady of the Lake," a turn-of-the-century, steam-powered ferry that used to run the length of Lake Memphremagog when the lake served as the only link-up between Canadian and U.S. rail lines for travelers going to and from Boston and Montreal. I recognized the print as the one I'd seen in the Wickerby photo album, hanging on the support beam just above Bex's head as she sits on the swinging couch, reading, a lit Christmas tree in the background where the oak table now stands.

I stepped up closer to inspect some of Albert's other merchandise: the sky-blue ashtray, the pairs of boots. The largest pair I figured to be Bex's father's or uncle's. The adjacent ones, all set out by Albert in neatly descending sizes, obviously belonged to Bex, her sisters and cousins.

WICKERBY

All at once, I was noticing pillaged bits of Wickerby everywhere. It was as if all the evidence of Bex's nightmare had been set out there in the brash sunlight before me. I was even suspicious about the lawn mower, remembering Bex storming around one afternoon six summers ago in a fit of rage about Wickerby's overgrown state, looking for the "goddamned lawn mower," which she insisted used to be kept out in the toolshed. That was the day she eventually persuaded me to go at the place with the old, dull scythe that still stands in the corner basket beside the bookshelves.

I stood there, surveying these remnants of past Wickerby days, thinking about how whenever the man downstairs in the house of refuse strays too far from his place, disappears with his shopping cart on one of his gathering missions, someone else with a shopping cart invariably comes along and starts to pick through his belongings.

Sometimes he'll get back in time. I once watched him run down a man who was just about to get away forever with the umbrella and the gooseneck floor lamp. Sometimes he has to replace a few things. One of these days, I'm afraid, a city sanitation truck is going to come by while he's not around and take the whole place away.

Bex—Ms. Anti-Possession, Ms. Possession Is Nine-Tenths of the Loss—has always relished this little give-and-take down on Lincoln Place, the idea of an ever-shifting, changeable house, as ephemeral as a spiderweb. But standing there in Albert's drive that afternoon, I wondered what she'd say when it came down to her Wickerby, wondered what she'd make of the fact that its caretaker has for years now, literally, been taking away her cares.

As for myself—a mere stowaway at Wickerby, a kind of pilferer in my own right—I was in no position to confront Albert. I just started asking prices. Bex's boots (her name was still taped to the underside of one of the tongues) and her father's (they fit me perfectly) I got for a buck apiece. The sweater I bought for two dollars. The ashtray cost a quarter.

I had decided to take all these items back here to Brooklyn with me, along with the diaries and the photo album, not so much as mementos, easy fodder, as Bex would see them, for earthquakes, but as further enticements for our return to Wickerby. If nothing else, I thought, she'll insist that we put the stuff back where it belongs.

Lucy waited in the car the whole time I was packing it up yesterday. Whatever primal impulses Wickerby might have stirred in her, she was all too willing to sacrifice them again for the creature comforts of her life back here in the city. I did, however, yank her out of the car after locking up the cabin, insisting that she accompany me on one last walk around the land.

I went down to the shores of Lake Y-Not. I then walked back up past the cabin and the top of the entrance road, past my withering garden and the trembling aspen, out through Blackberry Field. I walked first through the woods to the great tree burial ground, and then all the way up the hill to Bex's Rock.

It did seem a bit ridiculous, striding dutifully about those wide fields and woods, going from one far-flung location to the next, as though I had appointments there. I merely wanted to touch base again with the sites of all my lost standoffs, the places where I got so roundly outwaited, so gently rebuked.

It was almost noon by the time Lucy and I got back to the car. A porcupine was clinging to the very top branches of Rasteedy's butternut as I got in and drove away. It was as if he were trying to get the best view possible of my departure. The air yesterday had the same chill as when I first arrived at Wickerby. All around me, as I got out to close the sapling gate, autumn lit up the roadside trees from within. I listened to their rattling leaves.

It was surprising to see Albert's tractor parked at that hour up by his back door, the engine idling, and I would have gone up to tell him a last good-bye if not for the very peculiar scene unfolding there in front of his house. The members of what looked to be a very high-priced painting class, their Mercedes-Benzes and BMWs lining the road-side, were all stationed at easels in the morning sunlight, brushes in hand, staring intently in at Albert's farm, paint-ing it.

On and off throughout the course of the drive home yesterday, I'd think of him back there, trapped inside his own house—shy, petty-thieving, high-strung Albert—bob-bing and weaving and mumbling behind his blanketed windows, anxiously awaiting his capturers' departure so he could get back outside and resume his workday.

A MUMBLER TOLD ME ONCE that sometimes a stray bird struggles for hundreds of miles and many days to get back; that it returns in small, certain increments, having the city's patterned building grid imprinted on its brain: the encoded memory of little way stations where it can ride out storms and fatigue.

Bex and I saw a stray here late one winter night a few years ago, sulphur-crested, white over yellow over white, a color nearly too soft to see, huddled in a driving sleet on the sill of the bullet-hole-ridden stairwell window just outside our apartment's front door. By morning, it was gone, although sometimes now I think I see it in the comings and goings of the flock across the way, a flash of brightness in the prevailing swarm of blues and grays; not a bad life, in the end, for a bird: a top-floor apartment in this huge halfway house we've assembled here between the earth and the stars.

In the distance now, Manhattan has briefly claimed night's border again: the familiar, the nearly pronounceable glyph of that skyline. It looks tonight exactly the way I used to imagine it through that mumbler's eyes—as though I'm seeing it all anew; as though, like Wickerby, it is one and the very first house, multiplied.

On TV, the man in search of noiseless dawns is gone, but I'll leave the set on for Lucy. It relaxes her, like a warm flickering fireplace. Across the way, the pigeons have all come in, as have the mumblers and their flocks, and that woman with her dogs, and most of the rooftop picnickers.

The man in the house of refuse is back, checking through his belongings. He pats up at the air around him, then goes over to the square of stray cats and covers them with a spare blanket. Over at the fair, meanwhile, they've already closed up, and driven away with the Top of the World. I can see J walking back and forth, still watching over the thinning crowd, mostly kids now, heading off through the neighborhood's sidestreets with their prize goldfish.

It's strange. I see everything here that I had at Wickerby except that it's all in the margins: weeds limning the sidewalk cracks; trees gathering air from vacant lots; birds subletting rooms; cats aswirl at sills and doorsteps; dogs leaping rooftops; fish plying their portable ponds; the stars, briefly yielding again now to our show of lights.

At Wickerby, I was the marginal, the excerpted one, living in the least of houses, one that barely interrupted the day; just a loosely bound square of windows from which to look out on the ongoing absence of us; on the very darkness that first drove us to make over places like Wickerby in the shape of this home that I've returned to tonight, this thrumming, citied side of the world where even now the descending jets knit more lights along the edges of darkness.

Tomorrow, I'll wake to the clacking of store shutters and the whine of garbage trucks. Down below, the man in the house of refuse will start sweeping again, and J will begin making his mid-morning rounds among his fellow merchants. All the pigeons will be up—the mumblers' flocks and the mutts across the way—and that woman with her dogs, and all the other residents of the air city.

Out front, the construction crew will continue putting the finishing touches on the parkway—the promenade cobblestones, the gas lamp–shaped streetlights, and the wrought-iron benches. By the late fall, with any luck, we should have our street back for the first time in years.

Bex, I trust, will have returned by then and learned of my travels, too, to her Wickerby and of the plan to go back there next year and really establish ourselves, if, of course, Albert and the rest of the cabin's "caretakers" haven't made off with the place beforehand.

If you were to come upon it, suddenly, as I imagine those deer hunters or cross-country skiers do, you probably would think Wickerby a useless wreck and just pass it by. But if you did decide to take a closer look, to walk up to one of the cabin's buckled windows and peer in, you'd see signs of the life I've just lived there.

You might pry a window open and, moving past your own hesitation and the startled retreat of all the cabin's native stowaways, make your way inside and just stand there awhile. And then you could go even further, take my favorite seat by the window with the plum tree branches bobbing outside it, and begin to know that feeling of a moment's passing at Wickerby.

I think of it up there now, alone on that hilltop, tilting into winter, wonder if it will still be standing by the time we get back there. Until then, all I can do is phone, keep depositing the rings into that ongoing silence—little reminders of us and of our intended return.

I'll set alarms here over the coming months to remind me. Or better still, every time that man in the single-engine plane, whoever he is, flies over, and, wittingly or not, ties us into the long drone and seeming aimlessness of our lives, I'll go to the phone, dial that cold, rimless, northern night, and, with each ring, arrest, however briefly, the attention of whatever means to devour Wickerby—the woodchucks and porcupines, the mice, termites and the myriad unseen things.

I'll dial that dark, open hilltop. There'll be the crackling mimicry of distance in my ear, and then, around each unanswered ring, I'll begin to imagine all the twitched heads and wide-eyed stares, and the thick scatter of the rooftop crow, and the startled flight of the deer that had just then been rubbing its flank against the collapsing southeast corner, and its near-soundless hoof-squeak through snow.